SONNETS FROM THE ILIAD

D J Etchell holds several qualifications in science
and in classics from various universities. He lives
in splendid seclusion with his wife Jean and dog
Smudge in the North of England.

SONNETS FROM THE ILIAD

D J Etchell

Burghwallis Books

For Jean, Dawn and Emilia.

Contents

Preface

My initial plan for this book was to embark on what would have been, by necessity, a slow translation of the whole of the *Iliad* and to transpose my crude translation into prose, and then rewrite again in blank verse. I subsequently discovered, somewhat to my chagrin, that this had already been done several times and that published translations of the *Iliad* run into many dozens, if not hundreds. I decided on sonnets almost by accident; after the first few had been written, I realized that the method worked well, conveying the story fluidly and perhaps giving a sense of the marvellous poetry that is found in Homer. It also appears that this method of retelling the *Iliad* is a first.

I have followed the narrative within the *Iliad* closely; major omissions being those relating to exploits prior to the siege of Troy, as related by elders such as Nestor, and much of the detail of one-to-one combat involving the minor characters.

Most of the sonnets were written between February and August 2007. I remember finishing the last one, with some relief, on August 20th. Prior to that I had written two or three hundred other sonnets and much other poetry, mainly unpublished, ranging from erotic light verse, through nature poetry, up to very technically demanding things such as the double sestina. I particularly like the discipline which is demanded by the use of formal verse forms.

Long sonnet sequences are regarded as virtuoso—though, I suspect, little read—works in poetry. Starting with Petrarch's 227 sonnets dedicated to Laura in the mid-fourteenth century, the sequence surfaced in England with the 108 found in Sir Philip Sidney's *Astrophel and Stella*; this is the first true sonnet sequence in English. If we include only those sequences which exceed one hundred poems, we have Fulke Greville's *Caelica* (109), Shakespeare's incomparable 154 sonnets, and William Drummond of Hawthornden's *Aurora* (106); examples that were produced during the first flowering of interest in the form, around the final years of Elizabeth I's reign. Prior to this the restless and sublime genius Michelangelo had produced 78 sonnets, presumably between painting the odd ceiling and turning out various statues.

The sonnet has never gone out of fashion and closer to this century we have the 44 *Sonnets from the Portuguese* by Elizabeth Barrett Browning, so called because Robert Browning called her my little Portuguese due to her somewhat olive complexion. Dante Gabriel Rossetti left us a 101 long sequence in his *House of Life* and in the twentieth century we have the remarkable sonnet like sequence of John Berryman's *Dream Songs*, which runs to 385 poems. These were composed over about twenty years in four groups and are 18 line poems and thus not strictly sonnets.

The author thus realises that he is in very august company in presenting this sequence to a wider readership. The 317 poems within this volume may well be the longest, strict, sonnet sequence written in English.

A career in science meant that I did not start to learn classical Greek until I was in my fifties, so I did not discover the full marvels of Homer until that time.

I am indebted to two institutions for the opportunity to study in this area—the Open University and The University of Cambridge, via its marvellous tutors and facilities at Madingley Hall.

In writing the sonnets I relied heavily on the translation

of the *Iliad* by Richmond Lattimore, with some input from the Loeb translation of A. T. Murray as revised by William F. Wyatt. These were used to refresh my memory regarding the chronology and detail of the story. The *Dictionary of Classical Mythology* by Jenny March was also an invaluable aid in sorting out who was who and for invaluable background information.

I am frequently asked why I bothered to learn Classical Greek. The answer to the question is complex, and lies in part in the opportunity which became available. The motivation to grasp that opportunity lies, perhaps, in a lifetime of coming across texts in which bits of Greek are included, often with no accompanying translation, and the irritation caused by this, which I am certain must be shared by most non-classicists. See *Tom Brown's Schooldays* for example, or *Ulysses*—"Ah, Dedalus, the Greeks. I must teach you. You must read them in the original. Thalatta! Thalatta!" When such words were written in the Greek alphabet, I could neither understand nor read them (Thalatta means Sea).

D. J. Etchell

Book 1

1

The goddess sings of anger hear her song,
Of sorrow brought by Agamemnon's pride;
Of Chyses threatened, and of insults flung
Towards Apollo, who by deeds replied;
Destroying mules and dogs then fearful Greeks
With burning arrows from his silver bow.
For days those barbs of death, destruction wreaked,
Till Hera told Achilles all must know
Why the god his vengeful shafts had loosed?
Though Calchas told them; angrily replied
The mighty king, who then heaped low abuse
Upon a seer, who's truth his rage denied.
    The stage is set for what dishonour brings,
    Urged on by pride, unleashed by foolish kings.

2

Insults fly and anger rises high,
Achilles seeks the sword, whose blade would cleanse
This scorn flung by a king whose words deny
The greatness of a heart which vows revenge.
Athene's edict holds his rage in check,
And Nestor's council dulls his fury's edge;
Dismay descends: for would this quarrel wreck
The cause which joined all Greeks in honour's pledge.
The son of Peleus: his force withdraws.
A plot forged by the gods is taking shape.
Tragic deaths will settle all these scores
And vultures wait, where sightless skulls will gape.
    The thirsting dust waits, dry, on Troy's hot plain,
    For blood will quench this quarrel with its rain.

3

Briseis, fair of face, is given up,
To fearful heralds sent to claim what's due.
Yet Agamemnon drinks a bitter cup,
Dishonour's draught would give him cause to rue
That act, which took Achilles from the field.
The Greeks must falter in the battle now
Which needs his mighty spear and valiant shield.
Brooding near his tent he keeps his vow,
Yet sorrow comes because his prize is gone;
Through tears he looks upon the wine dark sea,
His prayers descend to Thetis in that gloom
Where shadows glide and fronds waft silently.
   Insult, anger, grief, and sullen pride,
   A god invoked—but will she be denied?

4

Thetis rose on hearing his sad plea;
Up from the sea, like mist, to hear his tale:
Of debt long owed and who had paid the fee
Of honour lost, of justice and betrayal.
His mother mourned a death which soon would come
And cursed the evil fate imposed by birth;
Now she must try a journey to the home
Of all the gods, to seek to lift his curse.
She knew that Zeus with all the Aithiopes
Must feast by Ocean's end a dozen days.
She bade her son hold fast, for yet she hopes
Her pleas will change what fate holds in its maze.
   On that twelfth dawn she rose up from the sea
   To beg that Zeus would alter destiny.

Grieving, Achilles sits, watching two heralds lead Briseis from his tent.

5

Meanwhile, Odysseus, in his black ship
Had brought Chryseis to her fathers arms,
And to please the god: a holy gift—
A hecatomb, arrayed in sacred forms
Around the altar, so the priest might pray.
Chryses, in his joy, then asked aloud,
The god to lift the heavy curse which lay
Upon the Greeks like some dark awful shroud.
Apollo heard his words and all day long
A feast was made, of roasted flesh and wine;
Though none could eat the god was praised in song;
His heart grew glad to hear the hymn divine.
      Thus satisfied the god sent homeward winds
      A bargain kept, his curse the god rescinds.

6

At last the twelfth dawn came and Thetis rose
To leap up from the waves to heaven's rim;
And there on high Olympus all her woes
She poured out to the god king, urging him
To give the Trojans victory until,
Ignoble, Agamemnon made amends.
The father of the gods sat brooding; still:
"I grant this wish and Hera's wrath descends".
Yet Cronus' son then spoke, and bowed his brow,
Assenting by that sign to what she'd tasked;
Then as the mountain quaked he urged her—go!
Lest his sly queen find out what she had asked.
      But Hera had not failed to see her come
      And mocked her lord to find out what he'd done.

7

Zeus then spoke and subtly put aside
That which Hera feared had taken place.
His anger caused her questions to subside;
She sat in fear of falling from his grace.
The gods were troubled at this argument.
Hephaestus said, to calm his mother's fears,
That mortals were not worth such discontent,
The gods should reign in laughter not in tears.
He filled her cup so feasting should begin,
And then to all he passed the wine filled bowl,
Apollo played, and laughter's medicine
Cured all ills and banished all their dole.
> Then Zeus went to his bed, all anger spent,
> Beside him Hera slept then, well content.

Book 2

8

Agamemnon, in ambrosial sleep,
Was lured to act by a destructive dream,
Disguised as Nestor, where night's shadows creep,
That phantom sent by Zeus then wove its scheme.
He woke; believing Troy would fall that day,
Buoyed up by foolish hopes the spirit raised.
He donned his kingly garb at break of day,
Then summoned all to share his dreamed malaise.
They gathered swiftly at the meeting place
And Agamemnon told them that the gods,
In unison, now backed them in war's race,
And victory was sure despite all odds.
  Thus blazing rumour, then, urged all to arms,
  And fanned the battle flame with false alarms.

9

The chief of chiefs held high that sceptre forged
By lame Hephaestus, symbolising might,
And wooed his eager throng with cunning words
And told them Zeus now urged all tribes to flight.
Their hearts were stirred like those long leaping waves
Which, restless, form on the Icarian Sea,
And homeward thoughts then gripped those eager braves—
Hope's moment melting dreams of victory.
Yet Hera knew what course was mapped by fate
And sent Athene down with thoughts of shame,
To urge Odysseus with hard words to sate
That hunger for home-fires, and dreams restrain.
  The peaceful swell turned on the cusp of war,
  The tide rolled on, then broke in battle's roar.

10

With wily words, the chieftain's men were turned
Back to that cause which tied them to their lord;
For honour binds and vows may not be spurned,
When claim is made by blood and sacred words.
All sat restrained apart from one, foul named
Thersites, whose bad, reckless chatter runs,
Reviling Agamemnon who he blamed,
Like some wild flood which calm and order shuns.
Ugly, bandy, lame, he there abused
Their noble leader, mighty king of kings,
Achaians listened as those words traduced;
Now from great Odysseus answer springs.
     Such baseness he put down with mighty blow,
     The fool in shame, in trembling fear laid low.

11

Thus laughter helped them lay aside concerns,
Hearts lightened as the babbler was brought down.
Odysseus then to deadly purpose turns,
Cajoling all with word and glance and frown.
Upbraiding them that they would put to shame
The mighty Agamemnon, lord of all.
He urged endurance; all had much to gain,
The ninth year's gone, thus Troy must surely fall;
That prophesied by Calchas must be near.
He then recalled the portent Zeus had sent:
The blood backed snake which took nine sparrows, dear;
They were fluttering years, and this the tenth!
     From all the ranks erupted a great cheer
     They praised his words and put aside all fear.

12

Geranian Nestor spoke of wrangling words
Which brought no answers to the conflict's claim,
Taunting them with insults, sharply barbed,
Reminding all of spoils and oaths and fame.
He asked them: "Could the son of Cronus lie?"
Then told them, "Those who left would never know!"
Yet those who stayed for honour or to die
Would gain those favours which the gods would show.
Then he sternly counselled his great king
To rank all, clan by clan, and tribe by tribe.
Thus with their kin the brave would seek to win
That glory, which is to the knave denied.
      The will of heaven soon must be revealed
        By victory or ruin on the field.

13

In answer to that speech, with golden praise,
Agamemnon lauded old Nestor,
Yet told of sorrows which the gods had made,
Of fruitless strife which turned his clans from war.
Regret was in his words that he had fought
With high Achilles over a mere girl.
Then he urged them eat for soon their sport
Must be with Trojans, where war's flags unfurl.
With their lord the Argives shouted loud,
As mighty waves against the crags, that sound.
Then scattering to tents they took their food,
And sacrificial fires burned all around.
      The son of Atreus, amid his chiefs,
        Prayed that day would give Troy to the Greeks.

14

Amid their prayers the barley grain was spread,
Then throats were cut as beasts were sacrificed.
Warm flesh was split and thigh meat, raw and red,
Was burned and favours from the gods enticed.
Though Zeus took all his due he would not grant
Fulfilment yet to Agamemnon's prayer—
'War's plot distils, until the gods decant
The victor's liquor from its brew's despair'.
Well feasted then the Greeks must take up arms,
Athene filled them all with strength to fight.
They answered to the call of bold alarms,
The field was packed with helmets gleaming bright.
      Blind eagerness for battle gripped them all
      They filled Scamander's plain, yet would Troy fall?

15

The clans were gathered; all those tribes were there
Which Agamemnon held as overlord.
From Tiryns, mighty walled, to Sparta bare,
From Arcadie and Hellas poured his horde.
The lists of chiefs seemed endless and the men
Were like those floods of leaves from autumn's fall,
Up from the ships their countless numbers ran,
In savage hordes, towards the Trojan wall.
The clans assembled ready for the fight,
Some roamed abroad, the land seemed swept with fire,
Intent was there, the moment seemed so right;
Did something lack in will, in hot desire?
      The Greeks advanced, their marshals must command
      Or lose the moment—as the gods had planned!

16

Now Iris warned the Trojans of the threat
From Greeks who came across Scamander's plain.
They marched in hope that now a nine year's debt
Would be repaid, in gold and slaves and grain.
Their dream was false, illusion lead them on,
For Hector knew that goddess, though disguised,
He ordered action, fruitless words were done,
All must, in haste, to arms or be surprised.
The squadrons formed upon the hilly mound
Which runs into the plain far from Troy's wall,
In separate groups their allies gathered round
Yet Hector, of the shining helm, lead all.
      The clans were formed upon advantaged heights
      Well armed, forewarned, brave hearted Trojan knights.

Book 3

17

Advancing Trojans came like shrieking birds
Which flee before a harsh storm's boundless rain.
The Greeks advanced in silence, without words,
Yet breathed out fury as they sought to gain
Advantage in that coming bloody strife.
Paris wore that symbol of the brave:
A panther skin, and took bronze spears to fight.
A challenge left his lips, yet like a slave,
When Menelaus answered it, he paled
And trembled like some craven caught in view
Of some great serpent, armoured, deadly, scaled,
Waiting vengeful there to claim its due.
      Thus, godlike Alexandros shrank to hide,
      From that lord who sought a stolen bride.

18

Ire now filled reproachful Hector's words,
Which heaped on Paris high disgrace and shame?
"Though fair, you gain the scorn of our brave hordes
Brought here to war, because you dared to claim
The wife of him whom you refuse to fight.
The gifts of Aphrodite are no aid
When battle's toils determine right or wrong,
Take courage and step forward with your blade!"
Then, godlike Alexandros hung his head,
Humbled by his noble brother's jibe
And vowed "now let us join, till one is dead,
Let Menelaus come, let steel decide!"
      All hopes were raised; one death could end it all!
      Could courage win or must Troy's towers fall?

19

Hector held his brave ones back from war,
Although Greek stones and arrows filled the air.
Then Agamemnon, shouting, strode before
His men to make them still, that they might hear.
Then poised between the armies, Hector spoke,
And told them that one duel may there suffice
To lift from all that conflict's heavy yoke:
A single death could rise in sacrifice.
Then, Agamemnon readily agreed,
And called for a white ram and a black ewe,
He asked that mighty Priam, with all speed,
Should come and with his name this oath imbue.
      Though all requested, rapidly was done,
      The fruits of those raised hopes would never come.

20

Iris sped to Helen in the form
Of Laodice, wife to Helicaon.
The purpose of her journey was to warn
The fair one that her lover's death might come.
She left her purple web of double fold,
To see those ranks which massed with unquenched spears.
The goddess caused old longings now to hold
A heart that had beat 'Paris' for long years.
Helen, weeping, sought the Scaian gate
And aged Priam called her to his side,
To ask of those who stood in mighty state
Among the war ranks, in their kingly pride.
      Odysseus and Agamemnon, those,
      Who swore a sacred oath before their foes.

21

Antenor confirmed what Helen said
And spoke about an embassy long gone,
Describing Menelaus, tall and broad,
And how Odysseus sat, as on a throne.
The speech of both he went on to compare:
Of Menelaus, clear, yet sparse in word,
Odysseus, thought by many of those there,
An orator as none before had heard.
Priam asked of Ajax, towering, tall,
And Idomeneus, Crete's high born lord.
She spoke of others, recognising all,
Yet could not see her brothers in that horde.
      For they were held fast in Lacedaemon
      By that rich earth from which she had been won.

22

The heralds came with riches for their lord:
Golden cups and wine, and fruit and lambs,
And then they made the aged king give word
That he must yield, to justly made demands
Made by the Greeks for Helen to return,
If Paris falls and Menelaus stands.
She and weighty spoils, the Greeks would earn,
Then peace would follow all back to their lands.
The sacrifice was made and lots were drawn,
To choose who first would loose his bronze tipped spear,
And Argives prayed for amity reborn
As both now donned their splendid battle gear.
      The gods decreed that Paris should throw first
      But all in vain; those solemn oaths were cursed.

23

A spear was thrown; one, vainly, was thrown back.
The sword of Menelaus on the helm
Of Paris then was shattered in attack;
His cry, in anguish, rose to heaven's realm
That baleful Zeus would not then give him best.
Enraged then Menelaus sprang upon
Fair Alexandros, seizing his helm's crest,
And whirled him round; fool, thinking he had won.
He dragged him choking back towards his men;
But Aphrodite broke the helmet's strap
And plucked him from that fate which waited then
And swathed in mist she, homewards, bore him back.
      Next she placed love's thoughts in Helen's head,
      And called her home to share her husband's bed.

24

Helen saw the goddess and then spoke,
In wonder, asking why she was deceived.
In vain she tried her pity to invoke,
Pleading that from shame she be relieved.
She asked for refuge in some other place,
Maeonia or Phrygia maybe,
Far from the war and hatred and disgrace
Which there, the gods had made her destiny.
All had seen how Paris, in defeat,
Had disappeared: dishonoured, thought his foes.
She asked that Aphrodite at his feet
Should take her place, renouncing godly vows.
      The angered goddess told her to return
      Or lose her love; an evil fate to earn.

Paris flees from Menelaus. Artemis is on the right and Aphrodite to the left.

25

The goddess led the way back to her home,
To that high chamber where her husband lay.
There Helen said, his valour might atone
For broken vows if he resumed the fray.
Then torn by fear she asked that he should stop,
Avoiding death, which waited for him yet.
Then lust-drenched Paris summoned her to play
And join him in love's bed, without regret.
Whilst they frolicked, Menelaus stalked
Amid that throng, to find his vanished foe.
The Trojans felt the shame his absence brought,
Now hatred for him, like black death, would grow.
   All saw who won the fight—up went the roar:
   "Now pay the price agreed to end the war".

Book 4

26

Hebe poured out nectar for the gods,
And goblets of pure gold were raised in pledge
For Paris had survived against all odds,
Thus Zeus let Hera feel his tongue's sharp edge
And malice filled those words which favoured Troy;
For if peace came her aims would not prevail.
Then fury filled her breast that with this ploy
The son of Cronus thwarted her travail.
Athene sat in fury, loth to speak
But Hera's breast could not contain her ire;
She urged: release the furies soon to wreak
Destruction, and pile high death's waiting pyre.
     The king of gods, perplexed, then asked her why
     Those gleaming walls her anger must destroy.

27

Zeus informed her—dearest to his heart
Was that city known as Ilion,
Yet fearing that the gods be torn apart
In warring strife, he granted it be won
But told his wife those cities dear to her
Would not be spared his anger, if he chose.
She said his whim, Mycenae, might lay bare,
Or Sparta, or on Argos bane impose.
The chief Olympian knew he must agree
And sacrifice old Priam and his lands,
Thus Troy must pay the price of jealousy
Which slighted Hera's vanity demands.
     Zeus, with grim reluctance, must obey
     And loose the dogs of war without delay.

28

Athene, then, was summoned to descend
And cause the Trojans, first, to break their oath
And by this evil to the conflict lend
New hate and purpose, lifting peaceful sloth.
In disguise she moved among the throng
And sought the well-famed bowman: Pandarus,
Then coaxed him saying, Wealth and fame belong
To him who kills the noble Menelaus.
His bow of Ibex horn was strung and aimed,
An arrow flew and hit the mighty chief.
Though flesh was cut, the gods and armour tamed
That savage shaft and saved him from death's grief.
      Agamemnon saw the blood, and groaned!
      He feared his brother's life flowed from the wound.

29

The king of Sparta spoke to reassure;
The arrow's tip no vital organ found.
Then summoned heralds came with herbs to cure
And poison to suck out and death confound.
Thus oaths were broken and the war resumed
With Agamemnon urging vengeance on—
Those whom the cloak of falsehood had assumed,
Those whom honour's mantle had foregone.
The chief of all rejoiced to see how full
Was war's new cup, which overflowed the brim.
Then regiments prepared while horses pull
Their chariots towards the battle's din.
      The son of Atreus commands; advance,
      With sword and shield and axe and valiant lance.

30

Idomene and the Iantes two
And other chiefs he found, all in good heart.
Yet wondered, with Odysseus in full view,
Why he held his troops, aloof, apart.
The lord of men rebuked the mighty chief,
For he had not advanced and waited now,
Reminding him: who leads the victory feast
Should be among those at the battle's prow.
Odysseus, angry at those empty words,
Assailed the king for thinking he was slow
To lead his valiant men with flashing swords
Into the war tide's ceaseless ebb and flow.
      His hasty words the tactless king took back;
      Odysseus sought his moment, to attack.

31

Agamemnon roved on battle rounds,
Cajoling or with seeming sharp rebuke;
Diomedes in silence bore those wounds
And yet the son of old Capaneus took
Them hard and said the hasty words were lies.
Diomedes said: "Silence now my friend
I understand what Agamemnon tries.
Do not let his strategems offend."
Then in full armour from his rig made leap
And on his breast the bronze made fearful sounds,
As on the shore when driving sea swells beat
When west winds drive and thunder's noise abounds.
      The war battalions ran like crystal waves
      Rank after rank, to glory or their graves.

32

Danaans then moved in silence to the fore,
Whilst Trojans in great clamour called, advance!
Athene, the Achaians lead to war
And Ares those from aged Priam's camp.
For terror comes and rout, as strife must rage
And groanings of the armies must increase,
As stout shields clash and first blood wets bright blade
And spear must slay, until night's start says cease.
Antilochus was first of those to kill
A Trojan there, his pointed shaft drove in.
Then Greek and Trojan fury had its fill
Of death as lance pierced chest and sword hacked limb.
>   Then blood, as winter torrents from great springs,
>   Flowed from wounds of hoplites and high kings.

33

Democoon, high Priam's bastard son,
Fell, by fierce Odysseus speared hard down.
Noble Hector, foremost in the van,
Gave ground beneath Apollo's scornful frown.
He roused the Trojans with a mighty shout
Reminding that Achilles did not fight.
Tritogenia saved the Greeks from rout
Demanding that they stand and keep from flight.
Bones were crushed and bellies pierced by bronze
With slayer slain, by comrade in revenge.
Thus Diores and Peirus, worthy sons,
Fell side by side, a death by death avenged.
>   Fierce multitudes, who into battle rushed,
>   By that day's end lay face down in the dust.

34

Book 5

34

Diomedes' bright shield and helmet blazed
With flames of glory, brighter than a star.
Athene placed him where the conflict raged
To show his valour mid the tides of war.
Two brothers—Phegeus, Idaeus,
Broke from the ranks, the first one threw his spear,
A miss, but now the son of Tydeus
Returned the bronze and cost the thrower dear.
The living brother fled with chariot
And left the other dead upon the ground.
Hephaestus' cunning saved him from his lot
By shrouding him in darkness all around.
      Diomedes then those proud horses claimed,
      From brothers two, one felled, one fled and shamed.

35

Hot anger then swept through the Trojan throng,
When they saw what came to Dares' sons.
Athene knew what needed to be done
To turn that tide: revenge, which often comes.
Thus taking Ares by his blood stained hands
Cajolingly she led him from the fray,
And told him sit by fair Scamander's sands
With winning words, far from that fierce mêlée.
Death then came by luck or skill in arms
As now the gods no longer interfered,
And princes killed their men in fateful swarms;
Both Trojan lords and Grecian chiefs were speared.
      And foremost, like a winter stream in spate,
      King Menelaus raged, till stilled by fate.

36

Diomedes charged, forceful as a storm,
To loose his power upon the Trojan plain.
Pandarus there, strained hard to do him harm
And bent his bow and then took deadly aim.
That bitter arrow pierced his shoulder through,
His corslet there was spattered with warm blood.
Pandarus saw just where the arrow flew,
Exulting, he called forth the Trojan flood;
The shaft had hit yet only caused a wound
And Sthenelos, then, pulled the arrow through.
The lord would live, his bloodied shoulder bound,
And soon his mighty efforts would renew.
     Diomedes had seen what had been done
     And vowed revenge, gods willing, soon would come.

37

Diomedes, wound weakened, prayed aloud;
The goddess gave him strength, and from his eyes
Removed the mist which like a secret shroud
Hid gods from mortals in their flesh disguise,
But she forbade that with them he should fight,
Apart from one, she gave him leave to spear,
The hated queen, the goddess Aphrodite,
Thus to the fray he charged in battle gear.
Like some fierce lion, wounded and enraged,
He thrust and pierced with lance and hacked with sword
The Trojans fell before this beast, uncaged;
Souls sent to Hades by that mighty lord.
     And there amid those chieftains he laid low
     He sought for him who fired the fated bow.

38

Aeneas saw then how his ranks were slain
As the son of Tydeus came on;
He sought among the Trojans one of fame,
The strong and blameless son of Lycaon,
And urged him: loose an arrow once again
At the god-like one, who now advanced;
But previously he had taken aim
And saw how through the corslet his shaft glanced,
Thus in despair he thought he faced a god,
Or one protected by them, standing by.
He knew that far away his horses stood,
He had no war-car now in which to fly.
     Aeneas said: "Now join, to fight or flee,
     Here in my well wrought chariot, with me".

39

Then in that car they rushed towards the fray
And Sthenelos could see them, wildly, come;
He urged Diomedes then, fast, give way
Lest to those charging two they now succumb.
His friend though would not choose ignoble flight—
'A hero's gold outshines the coward's dross',
He knew those steeds which came with hooves so light
Were of the strain which Zeus had gifted Tros.
Thus Sthenelos was told to seize as spoil
The horses, should Diomedes defeat
Those who came in fury now to toil
In war where death must come, or glory sweet.
     The four came, fearless, in their battle joy,
     Yet two would live and two must fate destroy.

40

The son of Lycaon cried to his foe—
"Diomedes, my bitter arrow missed
Yet now beware, an angry spear I'll throw
At you my feared and great antagonist".
The bronze tip pierced the shield and hit his breast
But there the corslet stopped that deadly lance,
And shouts of triumph turned to thoughts of death
For then a spear was raised to wait its chance.
And look! Athene guides the deadly dart,
To slice through fleshy tongue and teeth, and face;
To Hades thus did Pandarus depart.
Aeneas then sprang down so no disgrace
      Would be inflicted on his fallen friend,
      Whom he stood over, nobly, to defend.

41

Diomedes then lifted high a stone
And threw it at the son of Anchises.
The huge rock struck the hip and smashed the bone
Aeneas, hurt, then dropped down upon his knees
And Aphrodite with her pure white robe
Protected him, and bore him from the fight;
Whilst Sthenelos the captured horses drove
Towards the hollow ships in reckless flight;
Entrusting them to Deipylus his friend.
He turned back to the son of Tydeus
Who charged at Aphrodite, keen to wound,
And cut the peaceful lady of Cyprus.
      As from her veins immortal Ichor flowed
      The goddess screamed, and dropped her precious load.

42

Phoebus Apollo caught the lady's son
And rapt in dark mist bore him from the fray.
Diomedes called to the lady: run!
And shiver when you think about this day.
Wind footed Iris took her by the hand
To where her violent brother, Ares, mused,
She begged for rescue from that war torn land;
His horses then he could not have refused.
She fled back to Olympus there to find
Her mother Dione, that goddess fair,
Who soothed the pain and said that humankind
Could cause immortals hurt and foul despair.
      Then, Hera and Athene taunts began,
      Asking; "Was wound caused by golden pin"?

43

Diomedes then leapt at Aeneas,
Although he was protected by the god;
Apollo would not let his spear-point pass;
Three times he rushed, then four, as someone mad.
The god was angry that a mortal dared
To charge him so; thus with a mighty cry
He warned the fearless Greek he'd not be spared
If, foolishly, he dared again to try.
Then the son of Tydeus gave way—
A little—it was foolish to deny.
How easily Apollo's darts could slay,
His life preserved might later victory buy.
      The god delivered Aeneas to his shrine
      In Pergamus for healing's work, sublime.

44

Then wraith like as Aeneas, armour clad,
Apollo roamed through spears which killed and maimed
And urged that Ares from the battle drag
The one who's zeal the war god's pride had shamed.
The battle-god then urged the Trojans on
Disguised as swift Acamus, King of Thrace,
And Hector was rebuked by Sarpedon;
Thus stung by words he leapt into his place
And like pale chaff new winnowed from the grain,
When golden haired Demeter drives the wind,
The Greeks grew white with dust from Troy's hot plain
As wild hooves drummed down meadows, end to end.
  Around them Ares drew a veil of night,
  To aid the Trojans as they went to fight.

45

Apollo sent Aeneas back, restored,
To take his place as leader of his men.
All rejoiced to see their noble lord,
As battle came, they did not question then.
The two Aiantes and Odysseus
Stood with Diomede in war like pride,
And urged all Greeks to stand against the rush
Like mist unmoving on the mountain side.
Thus steadfast they withstood the Trojan charge;
Danaans knowing flight would bring them shame,
That noble deeds would house and tribe enlarge
And they would live in everlasting fame.
  Then Agamemnon struck down Deico'on,
  The first of those in death's new echelon.

46

Orsilochus and Crethon, twins of Greece
Were first of those by Lord Aeneas slain,
As two tall pines, hard felled by fate's caprice;
Yet death's fulfilment could not dull their fame.
Then Menelaus charged, his spear held high,
To save their corpses from the Trojan hands.
Ares' fury drove him on to die
Or live, while serving honour's high demands.
Antilochus ran swiftly to his side
Fearing hurt might come to his great lord.
Now two must fall or standing firm, abide,
Against Aeneas and the Trojan horde.
      Thus faced, the son of Anchises gave way
        Whilst those war-felled twins were dragged away.

47

The mêlée filled with thoughts of death and spoils;
Antilochus ranged wide and did great deeds,
And noble Hector led where tumult boils;
With Ares all around, the war-hate feeds.
Diomedes in fear could see who came
He urged that facing forward they gave ground,
To give way to the god could bring no shame,
Thus all retired while Trojans, close, came round.
Then Hector cut down two and in reply
Great Telamonian Ajax cast his spear.
Thus Amphius, gut pierced, was swift to die
And Ajax ran to strip his glorious gear.
      Then Trojans, loosing lances, drove him back,
        His mighty strength o'erwhelmed by their attack.

48

The son of Heracles, Tlepolemus,
Was drawn by deadly fate to Sarpedon.
Foolishly, he threats and insults tossed
And boasted how his sire sacked Ilion.
An answer swiftly followed then his word
As vengeance seeking spears were thrown as twins,
One wreaked destruction on that haughty lord,
The other left the Trojan's thigh in ruins.
Then from the conflict both were born away,
Tlepolemus a corpse to feed the pyre.
Death waits for Sarpedon another day
Yet soon his godlike form will feed the fire.
  A dark mist falls, that sharp shaft is removed,
  Then lifts as death by waiting fate's reproved.

49

The Argives slowly then, in ordered ranks,
Gave way as, grim, the Trojan legions came.
No back was turned at centre or on flanks
Yet many were by Priam's bold son slain.
Hera's fears grew then for those that died,
She thus recalled Athene to the fray;
She knew the strong attack must be denied
And to her war steeds went without delay.
Her chariot was set with fine gold wheels,
Which Hebe'd fixed upon the running rim,
And silver naves the axle's iron concealed,
Wrought gold and silver edged the carriage trim.
  Her car was ready where the proud steeds wait
  The sight is beauty—but the purpose: hate.

50

For dismal strife, Athene swiftly dressed
And donned her golden helmet with twin horns;
The awful aegis with its Gorgon crest
She wore to warn that death and terror comes.
She mounted high her blazing chariot
And Hera took the reins and lashed her steeds.
Then from Olympus they took exeat
To find that death-feast, where the war god feeds.
Thus through the sky gates, guarded by the hours,
Blessed on by Zeus they swiftly winged their way;
To wrest with Ares and his hateful powers
And with the men of Argos win the day.
      Two goddesses amid the battle's din
      Thus came to stir the flagging Greeks to win.

51

Athene sought the son of Tydeus,
To tell him she would go with him to war,
Where they would turn the raging battle's course
And by their spear work, Ares' efforts marr.
Athene thus put on the helm of death
So Ares would not know that she was there;
They found the war-god stooped, on blood stained earth,
There stripping Periphras, the mighty, bare.
Thus Ares saw Diomedes come near
And left the corpse and straight for him made way;
With fury, wild, he cast his deadly spear.
Athene blocked it, pushing it away.
      Diomedes now threw his javelin
      Which at his foe's fine war belt, drove hard in.

52

Then Ares bellowed as ten thousand men,
Whilst Athene's hands withdrew the spear
And as the thundery air he rose up then
To high Olympus, leaving all in fear.
There seeking Zeus he showed him where he bled;
The son of Cronos did not sympathise,
For hearing of his wound and why he fled,
He damned him for his hate and two faced lies.
And yet he would not see his son in pain,
Thus summoned Paeon fast to sooth and heal,
Then by Hebe, washed, restored again,
He sat near Zeus, no worse for his ordeal.
      The goddesses his murderous work had stayed,
      And thus returned to heaven's ambrosial glades.

Book 6

53

Between bright Xanthus and swift Simoes,
The conflict there was left to tides of men;
Without the gods it ebbed, then saw increase
As one or other side came on again.
First, Telamonian Ajax broke the ranks
Of Troy's battalions, cheering all his clan;
Diomedes and all the Grecian chiefs,
Came surging where the conflict's currents ran.
Menelaus: Adrastus took alive,
Who supplicating begged his ransom's fee
Be sought, that he at home once more could thrive;
But Agamemnon doomed that destiny.
      Saying none from Troy should rise from death
      Then with his spear he stopped that captive's breath.

54

There, Nestor cried: "Let death and terror rule
And give no quarter to our Trojan foe.
Forget your plunder, trust in slaughter cruel,
To teach these sons of Ilion what they owe!"
Subdued by terror, back they may have gone
But Helenus, the best of Augers, spoke
And Hector and Aeneas told, not to run.
But stand and hold all firm in battle's yoke,
And while they fought, to go again to Troy
To beg the honoured ladies—sacrifice!
Swift, to the temple, beg them, all deploy
With gifts, Athene's pity to entice.
      Hector heard his brother and obeyed
      And roused Troy's armies back to war's crusade.

55

They wheeled around and pushed the Argives back,
Whilst Hector left them as the Auger willed.
There, valour held them through that long attack
Until his urgent mission was fulfilled.
Then Glaucus, son of great Hippolochus,
Found the gap between where armies face,
Diomedes then asked him who he was,
A god or someone of the mortal race.
When Glaucus told him, then he realised
In times of old their forebears were guest-friends.
He smiled remembering deeds well elegised
By foeman then, who honour's debt defends.
     Then armour was exchanged, bright gold for bronze.
     Who asks its price when noble friendship comes?

56

Then Hector stood beside the Scaian gate
And women ran to ask of kith and kin.
He told them pray, though some had come too late—
For them sharp sorrows, deathly war gods bring.
Then Hector entered Priam's fabled halls,
With fifty chambers for his fifty sons,
His mother's greeting asked him, what recalls
My brave one from the place where war's tide runs?
Then spoke Hector of the shining helm,
Declining honeyed wine, which would bring strength,
He said that, "Troy, the Greeks might overwhelm
Lest gifts are laid upon Athene's plinth.
     Thus give to her the dearest thing you own,
     With twelve huge heifers, this may save our home!"

57

All the high born women, there, were called,
Whilst Hecuba went down to choose a robe,
For in that room were fragrantly installed
Rich wonders, which Sidonian women wove.
She chose the largest, loveliest of all,
And sought Athene's temple on its peak,
There that doom which hovered, to forestall
"Enter", said Theano, fair of cheek
And wife to the horse breaker, Antenor.
The priestess of the goddess let them in
And offered supplications from the floor,
That death's curse dark Diomedes might win.
> For innocents and wives she spoke in prayer;
> Athene turned her head and would not hear.

58

Then to the splendid palace Hector went,
Built by his brother in the citadel;
He entered there in anger, ill content,
To tell of that, which hard on Troy's men fell.
Paris sat un-armoured with his bow
Whilst Helen put her handmaidens to work
Hector said, reprovingly: "That now
Our people die whilst you your duty shirk!"
Godlike Alexandros, stung by words,
Vowed that to the conflict he would come
As quickly as slow armouring affords,
To follow where war's angry currents run.
> In silence Hector readied to depart;
> Could resolution fill that fickle heart?

59

Helen knew her husband's mind full well
And wished she had been won by better man.
She bade her brother rest from war's shrill call,
But need for action through his dark thoughts ran.
He left for home to seek his wife and child;
Andromache was nowhere to be found,
She walked Troy's walls with lamentations, wild,
Hearing that the Greeks were gaining ground.
On learning this he hurried to the wall,
There by the Scaian gate he found his wife
And she came running to him at his call,
Fearful of his death amid this strife.
  Andromache then let her warm tears run,
  Whilst Hector looked in silence on his son.

60

His baby was admired, a child of joy,
Scamandrius his name, which Hector used.
Astyanax, all others called the boy:
Lord of the city, chosen and approved,
For Hector had alone saved Ilion;
Yet there his wife's soft words were filled with grief,
Remembering her father Eetion
And all her brothers slaughtered by that chief,
Abhorred Achilles, he who waited still
Beyond the walls, who Andromache feared.
She begged him to remain, her wish fulfil;
To stay with her, she knew his death day neared.
  Then Hector of the shining helm replied:
  That shame would come if Troy's call was denied.

61

Hector said that Troy some day must fall,
And how that thought was nothing by compare
To that of his fair wife in Grecian thrall,
With all men dead, yet this ill she must bear.
Then he held his arms out to his son
Who shrank in fear back from his nodding plume,
Hector laughed and knew what must be done
He took his helmet off and laid it down;
Then lifted up his son and prayed to Zeus
That his small boy would grow to high renown
And bring great glory to their noble house;
But fate would thwart the wishes hope had sown.
      Andromache then took him back, in tears,
      And went back home with dark foreboding fears.

Book 7

62

Then Hector lifted high his crested helm
And once more readied for those ills of war,
His wife lamenting, in her woman's realm,
For now she thought he left for evermore.
Then Paris in his shining armour came
To where his brilliant brother lingered still,
And asked that for delay there be no blame,
For being slow his wishes to fulfil.
Hector said "Your battle strength is strong
But holding back gives rise to words of shame.
Now we must leave to join Troy's valiant throng
Or our great name might ever lose its fame.
      And if the gods should grant a victory
      They'd raise to them the bowl of liberty."

63

The brothers swept out through the gates of Troy
And seemed as that fair wind sent by the gods,
Driven hard to seek to vanquish and destroy
Strong Greeks and win against ill favoured odds.
Athene saw the two and swift came down
From high Olympus into Ilion;
Apollo stirred, from Pergamus's crown
And met with her as Troy's high guardian.
He spoke to end the hatred of that day,
Yet knew Troy's towers must end in desolation,
A respite with the dogs of war at bay;
A duel would bring all brief conciliation.
      Though clearly then, they Hector's challenge hear;
      None would answer, all hung back in fear.

64

Both sides were seated, none would venture forth
From mid the bristling spears and shields of Greece.
Then Menelaus growled a scornful oath
That he would dare and death or glory seek.
Achaia's kings then looked on him in pride
For all knew Hector was the stronger man,
There Helen's husband, fighting, would have died
The Greeks thus sought another of their clan.
Nestor stood and spoke of Argive shame,
Remembering the valour of his youth.
The champions stood then—all of those of name,
Nine came forth to test death's awful truth.
       Then lots were drawn to choose a champion
       To try his bronze against old Priam's son.

65

Agamemnon was the first to stand,
Diomedes and then Aiantes two
Idomene and Meriones grand,
Eurypylus and Thoas came in view.
Then Odysseus, man of many wiles;
Each marked a lot and cast it in the helm,
Prayers were said and on them high Zeus smiles;
Ajax was chosen—Troy to overwhelm.
Bright armoured he walked forward, smiling, huge;
Those Argives looking on him were made glad,
The Trojans trembled seeking safe refuge
Yet Hector's honour, thoughts of flight forbad.
       Then Ajax came on with his wall like shield
       The son of Priam, there, must die or yield.

66

Insults were flung, and swift flung back in scorn;
Hector tried his spear, preferring deeds,
Near through the seven fold shield its point had torn,
Then in return the lance of Ajax speeds
Straight through Hector's shield and tunic too.
Both tried again, advancing like wild things,
With bronze on bronze their contest they renew,
Though Hector's point against the shield boss rings,
That of Ajax spills dark Trojan blood;
Then Priam's son let loose a massive stone.
It struck the shield, but still the giant stood!
In return a larger rock was thrown.
  His shield was split and Hector staggered down,
  But bright Apollo picked him from the ground.

67

Idaius and Talthybius approached,
Heralds of high gods and mortal men,
There, holding staves of peace the two they coaxed
To end the fight as night was nearing then.
They both agreed to call an honoured truce
And parted friends, exchanging rich wrought gifts.
An Ox the Greek king sacrificed to Zeus,
Now to Olympus rich aroma lifts.
As Telamonian Ajax had the best
Of that days skirmish, honour was his due.
Glad Hector, home in Troy a while, to rest
For soon war's deadly toils he must renew.
  A time to pause for council, to conspire,
  Whilst dead are gathered for the funeral pyre.

68

Both sides, long, in solemn council met;
They needed pause from war and all its dread.
The Greeks agreed defences to erect,
A wall and ditch, before their swift ships spread,
To stop the wild attack of warlike Troy.
On high, wise Antenor addressed them then
And said the Greeks would come, all to destroy,
Unless with gifts we give back fair Helen.
But Alexandros would not give her up,
Though gladly he'd return her wealth and more.
Then Priam spoke to say: "This night we sup
Tomorrow, must Idaius to the shore,
  To ask for truce, to gather up our dead
  And tell them of what Paris has just said."

69

At break of day Idaius journeyed down
To give his message near the hollow ships.
They heard in silence, lords of great renown,
Till words of scorn left Diomedes' lips.
All roared acclaim and thus the herald left,
With pause allowed to gain the fallen men.
They lifted these in silence, hearts bereft,
And to their pyres with sorrow carried them.
And while night's final pallor edged the dawn
The Greeks, above the ashes, built a mound,
With sturdy ramparts, thus a fort took form;
On its far side a ditch was dug around.
  The tasks complete, the hollow ships are saved;
  If gods allow and Trojan ire is braved.

70

As flowing haired Achaians laboured hard,
From high Olympus all the gods observed
Those huge endeavours yet with angry word
The mighty sea-god, of men's works, despaired.
In their haste the Argives had no thought
Of prayers to Zeus, nor offered sacrifice,
This oversight his jealous anger bought;
Poseidon asked that they should pay its price.
At their task's end, with feasting, Greeks drank wine
And all night long in anger Zeus looked down
Then with the voice of thunder's gave his sign;
Thus all Greeks trembled under his dark frown.
      Green fear took hold of all, then on the ground
      They poured libations till they had atoned.

Book 8

71

Dawn's yellow mantle swept o'er waking earth
As Zeus commanded all the gods to meet,
And hold back from the war or risk his curse;
His whip would fall on those who dared to cheat,
Or into Tartarus they would be cast,
Through gates of iron and bronze into the pit.
They all stayed silent at his words, aghast,
That he should bind them so, with deadly writ.
Athene spoke in sorrow for the Greeks
Who thus must perish at his high command.
The great Olympian reassurance speaks,
Though keeping dark those secrets he had planned.
      Then keen to view the war his gold car wings
      Lord Zeus from heaven, to Ida's holy springs.

72

Through opened gates the fighting men swept out,
With fewer Trojans though in mindful need
To save their wives and sons and all from rout,
Replacing legions with high valour's creed.
Then fateful death was laid on golden scales
By Zeus and there the Greek side tilted down;
Their death-day weighed, thus soon in Hades' vales
Must wander those who now the fates disown.
From Ida's peak great lightning fire he sent;
Thus no Greek lord dare stand and hold his ground,
Pale terror fell on all in swift descent
And war's confusion, dread filled ears confounds.
      Though all went back, Geranian Nestor stayed,
      His horse cut down, his flight by luck betrayed.

73

Diomedes, aware of Nestor's plight
Called out to great Odysseus to stay,
But then Laertes' son maintained his flight,
Thus that of son Tydeus saved the day.
He found the old man, bidding him to climb
In to his well wrought car, with horses swift.
With Nestor at his reins, they there consign
All hope to fate, which others dared not risk.
Diomedes at Hector threw his spear
Which missed, yet struck his driver in the chest;
Eniopeus was Hector's charioteer
Who mid Troy's bloodstained dust gained final rest.
     Now Zeus must act or find his will suborned,
     Thus with thunder's blast that pair were warned.

74

Nestor thus advised a swift retreat;
Diomedes agreed, reluctantly,
For this would seem a cowardly defeat
Which all those looking on his crest would see.
The two then charged back through those Trojan ranks
Which clamoured loud and loosed their baneful spears.
Then Hector called "Look how their hero slinks,
A woman filled with shame, weighed down by fears."
Three times he pondered, turning back again
To try his spear against the Trojan lord,
And three times from the heights of Ida came
Dark thundered threats which could not be ignored.
     Hector heard good omens, charging on
     And called on all to follow Priam's son.

75

Then Hector, boasting, said what he would do:
He'd leap the ditch and put their ships to fire
Take Nestor's shield, the shining armour too
Of Diomede', thus raising high the ire
Of Hera who spoke angrily, of shame,
That Greeks had died despite great offerings,
The troubled sea god knew all shared the blame,
But dared not break that law made by their king.
Thus Hector pushed his foes back to the ditch
And might have filled all hollow ships with flame,
But Agamemnon rushed into the breach
And rallied men to fight or fall in shame.
  He prayed to Zeus to save the Greeks and wept
  As anguish through their desperate ranks then swept.

76

Zeus, in pity, sent a splendid sign:
A fawn brought by an eagle from afar,
Which to his altar did the gift consign,
A sight which told the Greeks—remember war!
They turned once more to try its savage art
And filled with courage brought the Trojans down.
Diomedes was first of all to dart
Across the ditch to kill his man; alone.
Then all the chiefs of Greece, determined, vow
To turn a near defeat, by hard attack,
Atreidae, Aiantes death will sow
Amongst those surging ranks, now beaten back.
  The Greeks have turned to stop the Trojan tide;
  But will they win or soon be swept aside?

77

Teucer there, with arrows from his bow,
Sent down chiefs of Troy to shadowed night;
The shield of Ajax sheltered him as now
Lord Agamemnon urged him on to strike,
And promised gifts, if Greece should ever win;
The blameless archer said, none were required,
That he was eager; thus amidst his kin
His deadly shafts against the foe were fired.
Twice he tried to bring wild Hector down
And twice he killed another standing near.
Down Priam's son Gorgythion was thrown
And Hector's friend his faithful charioteer.
       Now bitter sorrow, Hector, overwhelmed
       As grief closed round his heart for his dear friend.

78

Now Hector vaulted down and cried in rage,
Then raised a weighty stone up from the plains
And rushed at Teucer, madly, to engage
Him in that duel which ends when one remains.
Teucer notched his arrow—drew it back
But Hector struck him with the mighty rock
Before the bow could speed that deadly shaft;
The archer stumbled to the earth in shock.
Then Ajax stepped above him with his shield;
Two others came in haste to bear him back
To safety, by the hollow ships concealed,
Whilst all of Troy resumed its wild attack.
       Hector led the charge like one from Hell,
       Whilst Greeks, in rout, back to their dark ships fell.

79

The Greeks raised fearful voices high in prayer
As Hector looked to kill, with Gorgon's eyes,
Till Hera heard the Argives in despair
And told Athene of their desperate cries,
Yet she feared her father's edict still
And weighed the danger's, if she ventured down,
Defying thus the great Olympian's will;
She knew that she must dare his vengeful frown.
Then Zeus was angered when she whipped her steeds
Through those sky gates, guarded by the hours;
Thus with a message gold winged Iris speeds:
'To turn or feel the fury of his powers'.
       They dared not disobey that high decree
       And thus turned back in hopeless misery.

80

From Ida to Olympus, Zeus returned,
To take his place high on his golden throne.
Hera and Athene sat, concerned,
Apart from all the other gods, alone.
The son of Cronus asked them why they grieved
And told them what he willed must come to be;
Then warned them of their fate if they deceived
And tried to alter now his will's decree.
He said that godlike Hector's glory yet,
Would grow in blood as ranks of Argives fell,
Until that day to come, of dark regret,
When Achilles rose, as fates foretell.
       Then night brought down to Troy unwelcome rest
       But to the Greeks a respite, three times blessed.

81

Then glorious Hector scented victory
And as the sun went down called all to meet;
Dismounting with his spear so all could see
And hear those words—which promised harsh defeat
Would fall on those trapped by their narrow ships.
He ordered watch fires lit and all to feast.
Then, pleas of hoped for glory left his lips,
When coming Dawn would Troy's war hordes release.
Dardanians roared approval at his words,
Then went to eat and rest and sacrifice.
Thus hopes were high that soon with spears and swords
Their deeds could put the Argive ships to flight.

  Though fragrant scents rose up from Troy's dark plain.
  The prayers they carried, scornful gods disdain.

Book 9

82

Immortal panic gripped each Grecian heart,
Cold terror's cousin, rising as those twins,
Zephyrus and Boreas which start
In Thraces' mountains—West and Northern winds;
Which swoop and stir the darkened water's crest
To troubled motion with their squally sighs,
Thus sorrow filled great Agamemnon's breast
At what might come when dawn let day arise.
Betrayed by Zeus, he thought the Greeks must flee
Back to their father's lands in hollow ships.
Diomedes, with this would not agree,
Thus words of courage passed his warlike lips.
     He claimed that shame would follow their retreat
     And urged the Greeks to stay till Troy's defeat.

83

Nestor then stood forth, with council wise,
Suggesting food and rest before the day.
Agamemnon took this sound advice,
Then set the guards and lead his chiefs away,
To feast before they urgently took thought
On what must be their will upon the dawn.
Then Nestor spoke of deeds which now had brought
The Argives under mighty Zeus's frown.
Briseis was taken from Achilles' tent,
Dishonouring their greatest warrior;
Thus from the war with his dread troops he went,
His Myrmidons now idle on the shore.
     Agamemnon knew his wrongs and hence
     Promised her return, and recompense.

84

Tripods, gold and cauldrons, horses strong,
These entire he swore that he would give;
Admitting to Achilles he was wrong
And asking him to join them and forgive.
A daughter as his bride, seven citadels
Seven maids from Lesbos and the fair Briseis.
Phoenix went to that lords tented halls,
To ask him to return and take the gifts.
With him went those chiefs who were loved best
By great Achilles, those whom he'd known long;
Odysseus, it was hoped, above the rest
Would heal the rift and rectify that wrong.
      They walked those night sands where the dark sea runs,
      Towards the ships where camped the Myrmidons.

85

They found Achilles at his splendid lyre,
Clear sounding, played to put the soul at rest.
Patroclus stood there watchful by the fire;
All entered then, those chiefs who he loved best.
The son of Peleus rose then, amazed,
To see his friends, the bravest of the brave.
He ordered a great drinking bowl be raised
And then a greeting cup to each he gave.
Then meats were roasted on the embers red
By Patroclus and by Automedon.
The food was served on platters and with bread
With offerings they feasted, everyone.
      Then at its end Odysseus raised a toast,
      With wingéd words implored aid from his host.

86

Despite the offered gifts and subtle words,
Well woven by Odysseus in his plea,
Achilles spoke of battle's high rewards
Which justly came to all in victory.
Remembering, the prize from him alone
Of all the princes was demanded back.
The offer made could never thus atone
For insult which placed Greeks on war's harsh rack.
He spoke to all of Agamemnon's shame
And scorned the daughter offered as his bride;
He spoke of death, which gifts could not regain
And told them to return with their king's bribe.
      A twofold choice, god-schemed, before him lies
      Long life, forgot, or death immortalised.

87

Achilles said then: "Leave for home and peace,
For Zeus it seems now favours Ilion.
Go, lest hollow ships should come to grief."
In striken silence there stood everyone.
Phoenix spoke first filled with stormy tears,
Of how he was sent forth by Peleus
To tend the young Achilles through the years,
Recalling days when he, felicitous,
Loved well the child and raised him as his own;
He asked him thus to put aside his vow,
To take those gifts sent to him to atone
And in return the gift of hope allow.
      He said all Greeks would honour his return,
      To fight once more, lest all their ships should burn.

88

Achilles though, rejected all their pleas,
And said of man brought gifts he had no need,
For there obeying mighty Zeus' decrees
His honour held, through holding to his creed,
Which thus would keep him by the hollow ships
As long as life's wind stayed within his breast,
And though words of contempt came from his lips
He begged old Phoenix stay, a welcome guest.
Then Ajax seeing how the matter lay
Urged all to leave and quickly tell the king
How proud Achilles kept yet from the fray,
That gifts nor words no change of heart could bring.
      His heart still angry at his name's disgrace,
      Achilles stayed unbending in his place.

89

He swore abstention from that bloody fight,
Until the greatest of old Priam's sons
Should come with fire and try to set alight
The ships and shelters of the Myrmidons.
Then with deadly words he prophesied
That Hector would be checked, though filled with rage.
Then with libations; though not satisfied,
The emissaries left with that message.
Then in their host's great tent all went to rest,
There Phoenix lay awaiting golden dawn
And with Achilles Phorbas' daughter slept
And with Patroclus Iphis settled down.
      Thus with captive maids they rest content,
      At day, will sounds of war make them relent?

90

In hope the Argives greeted, with gold cups,
Those returning from Achilles' tent;
Then Agamemnon asked Odysseus
If that mighty war-lord would relent.
His answer filled expectant Greeks with gloom,
That yet his noble heart was filled with rage,
They pondered, silent, on impending doom,
For nothing could Achilles' hate assuage.
Diomedes then spoke of his resolve
And urged his king to rest until the dawn,
When their courage would war's problems solve
With men together, strong in ranks, close drawn.

They poured libations then went off to rest,
Each to his bed to sleep, by slumber blessed.

Book 10

91

In sleep's soft bondage all his men were kept,
Whilst Agamemnon pondered deep within,
In dreadful turmoil as the night slow crept
To dreadful day and coming conflict's din.
He sought out Nestor, son of Neleus,
With Menelaus, searching for some plan;
They needed Ajax, Idomeneus,
To wake before the council meet began.
Agamemnon came to Nestor's tent,
To tell him restful sleep was not for him;
He pondered their tomorrow, ill content,
Such are the cares and burdens of a king.
      Swift council came: prepare the Grecian hordes
      Let words of war make ready eager swords.

92

The two set out to gather all the chiefs;
Then Nestor woke Odysseus from sleep,
Reminding him of all their recent griefs,
Thus roused, he then set out with him to seek
All those war-lords sleeping by their ships.
One by one the leaders came as called,
To conclave, on clean ground beyond the ditch,
To plan how Hector's rage might be forestalled.
Wise Nestor said he needed spies to see
What those waiting Trojans had in mind;
This knowledge still could bring Greek victory,
Yet those who went would mortal danger find.
      There, all stood silent stricken by their fears,
      Aware hope hid amid sharp Trojan spears.

93

Diomedes, the brave one, then spoke forth,
Impelled to words by his great hearted pride:
That he would go if one more showed his worth
By facing those great dangers at his side.
Who disdains death it seems, high courage breeds,
Thus many offered then to go with him;
He chose that one renowned for wiles and deeds:
Odysseus, quick of mind and strong in limb.
They hurried, for the night was two thirds gone,
To arm and dress, to pass as Trojan guards;
Then setting off, Athene led them on
With Heron's cries and both used pleading words
     To pray for safe return from their grim task.
     Athene heard and glad, grants what they ask.

94

They journey like two lions in black night
And steal through corpses, war-gear, and dark blood;
Whilst Hector called his war-lords in that fight,
To likewise dare to find how Greek plans stood.
The first response, again, was silent dread,
Till Dolon said that he would dare to try,
With grey wolf's pelt around his shoulders spread.
He left to risk those Grecian lines nearby,
But keen Odysseus saw him as he came
And told Diomedes to let him pass,
Then they would turn to learn the stranger's name;
Their trap would close near to the Argive mass.
     They let him go a plough team's distance then,
     Moved back to take him near their sleeping men.

95

He heard their steps and stopped, and then he saw
The two who came were enemies not friends.
Then in despair his swift feet gripped to claw
The ground to lose those two pursuing fiends,
Who like paired rip-fanged hounds in sight of prey,
Hard on his heels, moved closer at each turn;
Diomedes called out for him to stay,
Or else the sharp bronze spear point he would earn.
The spear was cast—its purpose was to miss,
And thus with terror cause their man to quit.
The ruse succeeded—Dolon in crisis
Gave up flight and played his last gambit.
      There, green with fear, he pleads for ransomed life,
      Odysseus told him—truth would be its price!

96

Then Dolon told them how and why he came,
And sly Odysseus questions asked, of Troy;
Of where they camped and what was Hectors aim?
The trusting fool believed his wily ploy,
And told in detail where all tents were placed,
Expecting that those words would save his life;
Yet needs of war demanded that in haste,
They should leave before the morning's strife.
Diomedes thus clove him at the neck,
His head, still speaking, fell down in the dust;
They stripped the armour from the corpses wreck
And to Athene first war spoils entrust.
      And for that offered, asking in return,
      She point to where the Thracian camp fires burn.

97

They came to where the late-come Thracians lay;
Apart from all the rest of Troy's allies,
In slumber's depths, worn out by toils of day,
Secure, they thought, not thinking of surprise.
Odysseus saw where Rhesus slept, their king,
Near his swift horses, tethered by their reins;
He told Diomedes: "Here death we bring,
Now use your sword till naught of life remains."
They prowled as lions through low helpless sheep
Diomedes killed twelve and then their chief,
Who dreamed his final dream before that sleep,
Where death steals life, forever his to keep.
      Odysseus gathered all the horses' reins
      And whipped them ready for his camp's domains.

98

Odysseus stood, divided in his mind:
To run, or loot, or kill more Thracian men.
Athene told him hurry back or find
Some other god might rouse these sleepers then.
And so it was—Apollo looking down
Was angered seeing her attend the two.
He roused the Thracian lord of high renown,
Hippoko'on, who groaning at the view
Of ghastly slaughter, raised a clamour loud
And in that turmoil both the spies rode fast
To tell old Nestor what that night allowed,
Then all rejoiced that luck had turned at last.
      They bathed, then dined and rested well content
      And poured out wine for victory, god sent.

Book 11

99

Dawn arose then from the bed of Tithonus,
To carry light to mortal men and gods;
Zeus, in anger, sent down portents: ominous,
And strength to fight filled each Greek heart in floods.
Hate's goddess, in the centre took her place,
While all Achaians girded fast for war;
Thus readied, for its dangers to embrace
They stood before their ships on fate's dark shore.
Incessant clamour filled that morning's air
And Zeus sent blood, dark dripping down as dew,
Whilst all Troy's legions, fierce with hate, prepare,
Round shining Hector stood that hopeful few.
      Those lords who there, swift victory must seize,
      Or by the dusk descend into Hades.

100

Then like death's reapers lines of men advance
And sorrow's lady: Hate, watched all in glee,
Like wolves they turned with sword and bronze tipped lance,
Obedient to their god willed destiny.
As day increased then, both sides held and stood,
Until at last Danaan ranks broke through.
Agamemnon led that raging flood
Of deadly spears, which many would undo.
Bienor and Oileus went down,
Isus and Antiphus: Priam's sons.
Two sons of Antimachus of renown
Were caught in that red tide which deathward runs.
      They begged: take ransom! This was not to be.
      Their father's shame condemned, without pity.

101

Argives advanced then killing with the bronze,
Like fires which sweep through forests on the wind,
Surging forth with death, whose dark tide runs
Up to the Scaian gate as was destined.
There it faltered near the sacred oak,
For then the Trojans turned and held their ground;
To Hector, Iris, hopeful war-words, spoke:
That soon the rampant surge would turn around.
She told him Zeus commanded he should hold
Until a spear would Agamemnon wound,
And then his power to kill would gods uphold,
Until dusk came his war cry would resound.
      She promised he would reach the strong benched ships,
      But victory's promise never passed her lips.

102

The son of Atreus came on and on
And cut down Iphidamas huge and brave;
Then Co'on, who was Antenor's first born,
To Agamemnon's arm a spear wound gave.
Though hurt he struck back underneath the shield,
With spear and brought the hopeful Trojan down;
Though wounded Agamemnon would not yield,
Till weak from blood loss he could not go on.
He called on all the Argives to defend
The hollow ships, while he made swift return.
Thus weary from those wounds his efforts end
And Hector saw that now had come his turn.
      He urged his allies: "Come, with fury fight,
      For glory will be ours until the night!"

103

Hector, like some dark god, went before
All others, as a storm cloud on the sea
Which swoops to stir calm waters up to war;
Fulfilling thus his granted destiny.
He surged upon the Greeks as whirlsome winds
Which batter clouds, so bulging waves roll hard
And scatter as his blasting force descends
With havoc on the fleeing Greek rear guard.
Odysseus saw they neared the hollow ships
And called Diomedes: "Now with me stand!"
They turned and their bright spears from Troy's host stripped
Much life and purpose from that warrior band.
       Like boars that turn, when loud the horn resounds,
       They respite gained from those pursuing hounds.

104

The son of Cronos held the battle's reins,
And for the moment each side held its ground
And killed each other midst the turmoil's strains,
Which heaved with death as bronze each victim found.
Hector saw the Argive champions kill
And rose against them with a mighty cry,
Diomedes, Odysseus—felt the thrill
Of fear, yet vowed to stand and not to fly.
Then Tydeus' son, swift threw his balanced spear
And struck the high peak of the Trojan's helm;
It did its work, though dreadful death came near,
Protecting him from Hades waiting realm.
       Hector, stunned, took pause to clear his head;
       Diomedes had hoped that he was dead.

105

Hector rose and ran back to the fray;
Diomedes called him a Trojan dog
And promised, in close fight, to have his way,
If he too was favoured by some god.
He turned to strip his spoils from Paion's son;
There Alexandros, saw him kneel off guard,
He fired his bow and watched the arrow run
Clean through his foot and in the ground drive hard.
Then Paris, laughing, mocked and wished he'd killed
That lord who scorned the words of one who fought
In safety, from a distance, like a child;
Who had no courage when close trial was sought.
     Diomedes in pain then must retire;
     The Trojans had achieved what they desired.

106

Thus, spear famed Odysseus stood alone
Unwilling to retreat, he stood his ground,
For honour cannot come to those who've flown,
Then all the baying Trojans swept around.
Their trap though made a wound within their ranks
As when young men with hounds surround a boar,
Which rushes from his lair with grinding fangs
To fill the woods with broken limbs and gore.
Odysseus stabbed at Deiopites first
And Tho'on then, and Ennomus brought down,
Two others felt his spear point's deadly thirst
Chersidamas; Charops of high renown.
     His brother, Socus, stood and made a vow,
     He swore that death must bring one of them low.

107

He stabbed Odysseus' shield right through its boss,
The point crashed through his corselet, tearing skin;
Though wincing at the deadly thrust's raw force
He knew that wound would not bring death to him.
Then he drove his spear right through his foe
And, thunderously, mighty Socus fell.
Odysseus vowed that, there in death's shadow,
Vultures soon would feast upon his shell.
The Greek lord drew his spear out from the flesh
And Trojans saw dark blood and made a rush,
He called on all his friends to quickly dash
And rescue him from that Dardanian crush.
      Menelaus three times heard him cry
      And said to Ajax: "To him we must fly".

108

They charged, and found the Trojans crowded round
As dogs that wait to tear a wounded stag;
Though that pack their stricken foe surround,
He held them off with spear, held high to stab.
Now Ajax comes to stand with wall-like shield
And fight beside him till the Trojans flee;
Then Menelaus led him from the field,
And Ajax ran to claim, in lives, his fee.
He, like a swollen river filled with rain
Tore Trojans down as fallen oaks or pine,
Then in death's currents, carried from the plain,
They were swept as driftwood on the brine.
      In that tumult Ajax ranged far, then,
      His glory measured in his toll of men.

109

Though Ajax wandered far he did not meet
Brave Hector fighting on Scamander's banks.
Though he charged, his foe would not retreat;
Till Alexandros seeing in those ranks,
Machaon, letting fly with three barbed shaft.
Concern was great at their great healer's wound,
They knew the value of his skilful craft,
Thus Nestor drove across the bloodied ground
To take him safe, back to the hollow ships;
Then Kebriones urged that Hector drive
Where Ajax with his seven fold shield outstrips
All there, in valour, holding back Troy's tide.
      Though Hector strained to plunge into the fight,
      He wisely shunned the Telamonian's might.

110

Ajax drew back from the battle's sway,
For Zeus had cast dark fear around his mind;
Unwilling, yet he knew he must give way
To save the hollow ships, stood with his kind.
Thus Ajax paused beneath a rain of spears,
Eurypylus, who saw this, ran in aid
And though with bronze he cost the Trojan's dear,
An arrow loosed by Paris this repaid.
Thigh-wounded then he drew back to the host,
Yet called on all to help his mighty friend;
They stood with shields, defiant, at the slope
Till Ajax joined those ranks, which ships defend.
      Achilles watched this from his vessel's stern,
      And mused: "How fierce the fires of conflict burn."

111

Achilles called Patroclus out, to learn,
Who was the wounded man who Nestor brought?
He thought he could, Machaon, there discern,
But was not sure amid that fierce onslaught.
Patroclus heard his call and then emerged:
'And this began the evil that would come!'
Go search for Nestor, lord Achilles urged;
He went to find that elder at the run.
In Nestor's tent then fair Hecamede
Mixed a potion, rich, with Pramnian wine;
In cups of gold they took it and with speed
Drank to quench their thirst as they reclined.
      They talked with pleasure then until they saw,
      God-like Patroclus standing at the door.

112

Nestor rose up from his shining chair
To greet Patroclus and to lead him in;
He bade him sit, but standing near the pair,
The Greek declined and said he came to win
The name of that hurt man Achilles saw;
He courted anger if he longer stayed,
And having learned it must return once more
To tell his lord, Machaon there was laid.
Nestor asked him why such sorrow came
To one who had no pity, nor yet cared;
Would he wait, while ships were sought by flame
And Argives faced Troy's spears, till none was spared.
      He said Achilles soon might fight alone,
      With valour great, yet all his deeds unknown.

113

Nestor then remembered how they came
To gather all Achaia's fighting men;
Into his father's house, brave spears to claim,
And how Achilles warmly greeted them,
And how Patroclus, eager with his friend,
Was urged to join the cause to vanquish Troy,
Yet he was counselled, soundly, to defend
Achilles from that rage which could destroy.
He said that still he maybe could persuade
The mighty one to join the battle throng;
Yet, if some secret prophesies dissuade
Patroclus might his splendid armour don.
     To cause the Trojan horde with great dismay
     To fear Achilles coming, and give way.

114

As Patroclus then came towards his ship
He found Eurypylus, with wounded thigh,
And felt his pain and saw the dark blood drip,
Then asked if spears could Hector's might deny.
He said: "This day of death haunts wretched Greek,
For all the bravest, dead or wounded lie;
The rest, in weakness, sheltered vessels seek,
For none could now that Trojan lord defy."
He asked for aid to get back to his men,
To get the arrow out and raw wound healed.
Eurypylus had needs more urgent then
Than that message which his heart concealed.
     The news of Argive peril thus must wait,
     Till his friend in comfort was made safe.

Book 12

115

The battle raged around the mighty wall
And Hector came on like some whirling storm;
Through volleyed spears, he answered battle's call
And led the Trojans in their angry swarm
Up to the ditch, where paused their frightened steeds.
Polydamus then urged they fight on foot,
And Hector, wisely, cautious council heeds
And leapt down from his fine wrought chariot;
All sprang to ground and in battalions, five,
They charged the wall, well lead by lords of war.
In eager ranks to gain the way they strive,
Up to the wall in reckless hordes they pour.
   There with desperate spears the Argives wait,
   To live they must withstand this Trojan spate.

116

Yet one stayed mounted for the charge they made,
Asius the son of Hyrtacus.
Fast driving at that gated palisade,
He saw one open, where the Greeks might cross,
He thought that its defenders would not hold,
Thus lead his men, in careless mind, to doom;
For there stood Argives, two, both brave and bold.
These like wolves would soon their prey consume.
High hearted sons of shining Lapithai.
Leonteus, Polypoetes—named
And at their hands now many men must die
As bronze scars armoured bronze, in grinding screams.
   Asius groaned and praying beat his thighs,
   Zeus in Hector's cause, those prayers denied.

117

At all the gates the desperate Greeks fought hard,
Though with no joy as all their gods despaired.
Though Trojan killing came on yard by yard
Hector paused, till came a mighty bird,
An eagle, which, a blood red serpent held:
This writhed and struck the bird and broke away
And fell to earth, thus all of Troy beheld
That portent of great Zeus with much dismay.
Polydamus told Hector: "This brings ill!"
A sign that they could not complete their task;
But Hector raged that he would have his will,
To burn the ships no matter what the risk.
   Then Zeus sent down a blast from Ida's peaks,
   This sign which gave Troy hope, deceived the Greeks.

118

The Trojans then worked hard to breach the wall
And tore projections—broke down battlements;
The fierce Danaans would not let it fall
But laboured to extremes in its defence.
They, hides of oxen on the ramparts placed,
Then flung down spears and rocks on those below;
The two Aiantes up and downwards paced,
Urging all to pour death on the foe.
Thus like the snowfall in incessant rain
Their missiles wrapt the air in deadly shrouds,
Like sweeping drifts, unstoppable, they came,
Like icy squalls in ever deeper crowds.
   And through those ramparts Troy might not have won
   Had not then Zeus sent forth great Sarpedon.

98

119

The son of Zeus then like a wild thing came,
His shield held high, of flame bright beaten bronze.
There, as a mountain lion seeking game,
With spears to tear soft flesh, the hunter comes.
As warlike spirit drove on Sarpedon
He called to Glaucus: "Stand now at my side!"
They lead his horde of Lycians straight on;
Menestheus then feared that coming tide
And sent Thoötes running swift for aid,
"Summon Ajax quickly now," he cried,
"For here the main attack of Troy is made;
With help their entry may yet be denied."
      Telamonian Ajax heard his call
      And called on Teucer, "Come, to save the wall!"

120

First Epicles, the light of foot, was felled,
Struck down by Ajax with a jagged stone.
Then Teucer, with an arrow, Glaucus stilled;
With arm sore wounded he must now stand down.
Sarpedon, though downcast, killed his man
Then reached and pulled the ramparts leading edge;
It came away and now a pathway ran
Defenceless, just beyond the bastion's ledge.
Teucer rushed with Ajax, fierce, to kill
Great Sarpedon, with arrow or with spear,
The death they bore was stopped by Zeus' high will
To save, for now, the son he held so dear.
      Though Lycians rushed swift into the fray
      The Argive ranks held firm, not giving way.

121

The battlements thus formed a boundary line,
Across which both sides hacked and hewed at limbs.
Though flesh was torn and blood spilled on death's shrine,
And, without pity, rose harsh battle hymns,
The fight stayed balanced, even, on those scales
Like those held by a widow weighing wool,
Great care about the beam that work entails,
To serve the need which sees small bellies full.
Then Hector broke the impasse, driving on,
For Zeus now swept great glory in his wake,
Troy's charging pack with him the ramparts won
As he smashed down that door, which none could break.
      Hector's eyes flashed fire, his face as night,
      Brought terror which put all the Greeks to flight.

Book 13

122

When Zeus had driven Troy's men near the ships,
He left them in the random toils of war.
His aim fulfilled, his gaze from conflict slipped
To many peopled lands, spread out afar.
That other gods would come was not in mind;
Poseidon though had watched the battle run;
From timbered Samos down he quickly climbed
To Aegae, where his house shone like the sun—
Imperishable gold, lost in the depths.
There he harnessed all his fastest steeds,
Then drove his car across the waves high crests
Down to his cave, lost in the dark frond weeds.
  Midway between Imbros and Tenedos
  His horses grazed amid the green sea moss.

123

Towards the ships Poseidon quickly went,
For there the Trojans gathered like a flame;
They followed Hector, grim in their intent,
All raging forth to death or deathless fame.
The shaker of the earth rose from the depths
To stir the Argives, taking Calchas' form.
Both Aiantes, eager for war's wrath,
Then filled with valour looked on Troy with scorn.
Poseidon, swift, took on a hawklike shape
And rose and thus the pair his nature knew;
Then with joy they both of conflict spake,
For courage in their hearts had grown anew.
  Behind the two the Greek battalions turned,
  For where despair had lived, a new hope burned.

124

Poseidon, there, called out these wingéd words:
"Shame on you Argives, you young fighting men."
He rallied all to take up spears and swords
And said: "How strange, that Troy's few troops condemn,
The many, who till now were fierce as wolves,
Or leopards, hunting them like timid deer;
The strife between your chiefs no moan resolves,
Thus Greeks must rise in arms with danger near."
He rallied all to heed the needful call,
To fight or some great evil would descend,
"For Hector's through our gate and past the wall
And all must now the hollow ships defend."
      Battalions round the two Aiantes form,
      Resolved to push back Troy's approaching storm.

125

Spear-dense fury packed the battle line
As brilliant Hector's men were faced by Greeks.
Then courage with a desperate need combine
To give each side the victory it seeks.
Hector thought at first he might prevail
But spear thrusts by Achaians drove him back.
He called on all to stand and not to fail,
In their dire need to drive home the attack.
Deiphobus then came striding: Priam's son,
His purpose high, yet Meriones' spear
Hard struck his shield and death's prize almost won,
It caused the Trojan's heart to shrink in fear.
      Deiphobus lived, but with his hopes deterred
      Back safe amid the ranks he then repaired.

126

Mid rising clamour all the rest fought on;
Teucer was the first to down his man,
Imbrios, by marriage Priam's son;
Then Hector's spear at watchful Teucer ran,
Yet missed that Greek and struck Amphimachus.
Though Hector charged, great Ajax thrust his lance
And stopped him with the point in his shield's boss,
The ghastly bronze there missed its deadly chance.
Amphimachus was dragged off by the Greeks
Yet Imbrios could not be saved for Troy,
All watched then as his corpse a victor seeks
To strip its armour, defile, and destroy.
>   The lesser Ajax severed head complete,
>   And threw it in the dust at Hector's feet.

127

Poseidon, angered at his grandson's death,
Went forth to stir disaster for the foe,
And said to Idomené in wrathful breath
That he who lingered shame and fear would know.
The god disguised as Thoas called for speed,
The Cretan lord thus put his armour on
And like a bolt from Zeus then ran to heed
The call to arms from mighty Poseidon.
His henchman: Meriones, next he met
And asked him why, unhurt, he'd left the fray.
He told him that he came, though with regret,
To fetch a spear to hold the foe at bay.
>   In urgent haste for war the Cretan lord
>   Then told him: take a spear from my large horde!

128

Like Ares, god of war, led on that lord
As though with Terror, his beloved son.
So full of strength and dauntless, in accord,
To stand together till the day was won.
Meriones then asked Deucalides
Just where the Greek array was hardest pressed,
For there, their spears would serve Achaian needs;
Thus they took their stand towards the left.
Idomeneus came like a flame,
In valour, armoured, with Meriones.
The Greeks then rallied in war's deadly game,
To stand with these and meet their destinies.
      Thus by the vessel's sterns a great fight rose,
      As when a screaming storm the whirlwind blows.

129

The fight's confusion whirled in a mad cloud
Disordered, like dust swirled up by the wind,
The sharp bronze promised death amid that crowd
For many then for Hades were destined.
The lead was taken by the lord of Crete,
Though grizzled, he brought panic down on Troy.
Othryoneus—first met defeat;
His need to win Cassandra, meant, destroy—
All Greeks, to win from Priam her soft hand.
Idomeneus then seized his foot
To drag him, dead, amid the Grecian band
And Asius who tried to bar his route,
      Speared through the chin, lay, roaring on the ground
      And clawed the bloody earth, with awful sound.

130

Antilochus then slew the charioteer
And seized the horses, driving them away.
In sorrow, great Deiphobus had come near,
On seeing how great Asius, there, lay.
At Idomeneus he cast his shaft,
Which missed, yet killed another in his stead,
He mocked the Argives that his warlike craft
Gave Asius an escort to the dead.
Antilochus bestrode the fallen man
Till two companions bore him, groaning, back
To shelter from that conflict fast they ran
Back to the ships and safe from Troy's attack.
　　　Yet Idomeneus came on and on,
　　　And mocked Deiphobus, killing three for one.

131

Deiphobus pondered darkly, if alone,
He should face the Cretan lord in fight?
Or seek another from his Trojan home
To try to send that lord to endless night.
It seemed Aeneas best would fill that need
To aid him, thus he told him what had passed.
In anger then the high lord came at speed,
To test the Cretan; bronze against bronze matched.
Sure in strength the elder held his ground
Like some great boar which, wildly, its tusks bares
And yet he called his friends to gather round
Aeneas had war's gifts and those of years.
　　　Troy's lord then called forth, Paris, Agenor
　　　And high Deiphobus, masters all of war.

132

With gladdened heart Aeneas took the lead
Of all who came to fight with their long spears;
Lord sought lord, so eager in war's need,
To use the bronze to steal away youth's years.
Aeneas with his first cast missed his prey
Yet with his spear brought down Oenomaus,
Who fell, his fingers clawing in the clay,
His entrails spilling from his shattered corpse.
With spear retrieved the Cretan lord fell back;
Deiphobus cast, the aim was flawed again,
Ascalaphus though felt its deadly blast
And fell, to claw the dust in burning pain.
  Deiphobus then tore at the shining helm
  Of him who had just found the shadowed realm.

133

Then Meriones, running to avenge,
Plunged his spear in Deiphobus' arm.
Polites bore him to the conflict's fringe
To safety near his horses, safe from harm.
The rest fought on and many brave ones died,
Antilochus was first among the fray,
Against him many Trojan spears were tried
Yet Lord Poseidon turned their points away.
Then as he saw his safety in retreat,
Meriones took at last his chance
And drove his spear where groin and navel meet,
Antilochus, there writhed upon his lance.
  Till Meriones out the weapon prized
  And mists of darkness closed about those eyes.

134

Helenus with his sharp Thracian sword
Struck Deipyrus, hard, and rent his helm;
There life's commotion into stillness poured
As his blood ebbed he sank into death's realm.
Then Menelaus sprang to the attack
As Helenus let loose a shaft, to kill.
The arrow struck the corselet yet sprang back
Like chaff swept sideways at some winnower's will.
The javelin's dread point though found its mark
And pierced the son of Priam through his hand;
Thus he retired, amidst the host to lurk
Away from death, safe in the Trojan band.
      There Agenor drew out that deadly shaft
      And dressed the wound with wise and healing craft.

135

Peisandrus then came straight at that Greek lord,
But evil fate had marked him for his end;
His spear at Menelaus he drove hard,
He failed though, through the shield his lance to send.
Its shaft was shattered, thus with angry sword
Menelaus sprang at Peisandrus,
Who drew his axe behind his shield's sure guard,
They struck together, deadly blades across.
The axe came down upon his helmet's horn,
Thus Menelaus lived to see his home,
His sword drove through his foe's strong guard with scorn
And near the nose it smashed hard through the bone.
      Into the bloody dust fell both his eyes,
      And nothingness their orbit now descries.

136

Menelaus placed his victor's heel
Upon that corpse where all life's dreams had ceased.
He said: "Soon Zeus his anger will reveal
And send Troy hungry from this battle-feast."
He spoke of their unsated appetite
For war and of their vanity and shame,
Which some day all the great gods would put right
By wiping out their haughty race's stain.
Then Menelaus stripped the body bare
Of armour, which he gifted to his men;
Harpalion was next of them to dare
His bronze against that mighty Greek lord then.
      He stabbed the shield and then shrank back in fear
      Among the host, so death could not come near.

137

Bold Meriones let an arrow fly
Which hit Harpalion, hard by the bone;
It pierced the bladder, thus in agony
He gasped out life as dark blood drenched the loam.
The Paphlagonians lifted up the corpse
And bore him back to sacred Ilion;
There his father wept with hard remorse
That no man-price was offered for his son.
Then angry Paris fired at Euchenor,
A deadly arrow, striking near the jaw.
It brought that darkness which all men abhor,
Where light must turn to shadow evermore.
      Then back and forth the conflict raged like fire
      In blind confusion 'cross that bloody mire.

138

Hector did not know, that to the left,
His men were falling to Achaian spears;
Poseidon urged Greeks onward with no rest,
To send the Trojans to their waiting biers.
Yet Hector held the rampart and the gates,
For none could quench his brilliant battle flame.
Before him each Greek war-chief hesitates,
For they know death comes sure with that proud name.
The two Aiantes strapped in harness now
As oxen yoked to turn the fallow land,
That sweat and strain to pull the narrow plough,
Are bound together in their fighting stand.
   Came many with the son of Telamon,
   Yet with the son of Oileus, not one.

139

His Locrians lacked the armour to fight close
Yet used their bows and slings to strike at Troy;
In volleys from the rear their missiles rose
To rob Dardanian sons of battle's joy.
This may have driven back their surging ranks,
Had not Polydamus gained Hector's side
To urge recall of chiefs from all their flanks,
To meet and on new battle plans decide.
This council pleased him, thus he told his lords
To gather all together while he fought.
They rallied there to hear his wingéd words
Whilst Hector in the fray, his bravest sought.
   Though many dead and wounded Troy had lost
   Far on the left he found Alexandros.

140

Hector there rebuked his brother thus:
"Evil Paris, handsome, woman-mad,"
Then blamed him for the loss of Helenus
And all Troy's fallen lying, bloodied, sad.
He told him his destruction then was sure;
But Paris told him he was not to blame
And said that in the fight they would endure,
Then of those missing went on to explain,
That all were dead but for the wounded two,
Retired because of spear thrusts through their hands.
He urged that Hector lead the valiant few
In answer to their war-god's hard demands.
     They went to where the tumult's sounds were loud,
     Where toiled the bravest of the battle-proud.

141

They drove down as that storm-blast on the sea
Which boils the waves to ranks of frenzied foam.
There they closed and clashed but victory
Eluded them, wherever they did roam.
Hector like a murdering god led on
And probed to find a weakness 'mid the Greeks;
Then Ajax came to challenge Priam's son
And said: their spears denied the thing he seeks.
Yet as he spoke a towering eagle came
To his right hand as though the gods gave sign;
The Greeks took courage 'mid their toil and pain,
Yet Hector claimed the aid of one divine.
     He promised Ajax that his death would pay
     For insult, yet the Greek would not give way.

Book 14

142

While Nestor took his wine he heard war's bay;
He told Machaon, stay, to drink and bathe,
For he must find then how the struggle lay,
It seemed the foe was near to their enclave.
He left the shelter, saw the shameful flight
Of many Greeks as Trojans passed the wall;
He pondered, should he rush into the fight
Or search for Agamemnon lest they fall.
He took the latter course and found the king
With other wounded lords, next to their ships;
They thought that soon defeat would great Zeus bring,
Thus words of sorrow passed between their lips.
  That far from Argos all the Greeks must die;
  Zeus it seemed would Hector glorify.

143

Agamemnon said: "Come launch the ships,
Those in line, laid closest to the sea.
Let's place them where shining water laps,
Anchored safe far from our enemy."
Odysseus, looking darkly at him, spoke
And said that: "Ruin's words now pass your teeth."
Then begged him, 'words of sorrow' to revoke,
For dark dishonour travels with defeat.
Those words caused pangs in Agamemnon's mind,
And thus sought council from his many chiefs.
He asked if any, young or old, could find
Some strategy to end their present griefs.
  Diomedes proclaimed his warlike birth,
  And urged, though wounded, they once more face death.

144

Thus all obeyed and went back to the fray,
With Agamemnon leading all his lords.
Poseidon, as an old man, came to say:
"Wars tide will turn", and hope came with those words.
He swept across the plain with a huge cry
As though ten thousand rushed to hateful strife.
He bustled here and there that great ally,
To give them heart, to bring their hopes to life.
Hera of the golden throne looked down
From high Olympus, happy in her heart,
At how Poseidon turned the Argives round
To stand once more with pride at war's rampart.
      She saw Zeus sit amid high Ida's springs,
      And sought to turn his mind from war-like things.

145

She thought that sly seduction would distract
Her lord from what occurred on Troy's dry plain;
She marshalled all her soft arts to attract
By sweet beguilements, Zeus, to love's hot game.
Anointed thus with fragrances and oil
And dressed to lure in her ambrosial robe,
With rings and all those furbelows which coil
About the female, girding her for love.
She then sought Aphrodite with soft lies
Asking for those gifts which overwhelm,
Gods or mortals by desire's surprise,
To go to Oceanus in his realm,
      His and Tethys quarrel to resolve,
      And by love's arts their enmity dissolve.

146

Aphrodite, smilingly, agreed—
Unwrapped the splendid Zone which held her breasts.
There are found love's splendours, filigreed,
And all those sighs and raptures which rule sex.
The Owl-eyed lady, Hera, smiled and left
With speed, to Lemnos urgently to seek
Death's lesser brother, with a sly request—
Love's labours ended, then should enter—Sleep.
She promised him a throne of shining gold,
Made by Hephaestus and a footstool too;
Yet Sleep demurred, he knew her wiles of old,
And Zeus might blast him, if of this he knew.
      She promised fair Pasithea to him,
      The Grace in bribe, his subtle aid to win.

147

Sleep, though pleased, demanded: "swear by Styx!
By its dread waters, ineluctably
With hands on earth and sea your oath will fix,"
She gave her sacred word about his fee;
Swearing by those Titans in the pit.
Then mantled in grey mists they swiftly went,
To Ida where streams start, where sweet springs sit.
Then Sleep awhile, amid the pines was sent,
Whilst Hera made her way to Gargarus,
There, with guile, her lord's lulled mind to plunder
To wrap him in her secret web of lust
And in their bed, constrained by love, to linger.
      His mind was swamped by scented, sweet desire,
      All thoughts of war consumed in love's mad fire.

148

Filled with need, Zeus asked why she had come.
Hera lied and said: "To end discord,
She travelled to find Tethys, to reclaim
That love which once had bound her to her lord.
She'd come to tell him she was on her way
To visit Oceanus in those deeps,
At this earth's ends, far from the light of day."
Now Zeus, enamoured by her presence, speaks:
"Go there later, come with me to bed!
For you, above all others I desire.
Wild passions surge now, like a mighty flood,
My heart is melting, burning in love's fire."
   Thus Zeus by Hera's cunning was induced
   To want her more than all those he'd seduced.

149

Zeus listed all his lovers, one by one,
Europa, Leto fair and Semele,
Sweet stepping Danäe, wife of Ixion,
Demeter and the Theban, Alcmene.
He swore none any way came near to her.
Thus Hera promised, with soft guile, to lie
Beside him if no other was aware;
She, his hearts' desire could not deny.
Then Zeus around them closed a golden cloud
And took up Hera in his lustful arms.
Below the earth sprang fresh with flowers to crowd,
A world made fertile by the love god's charms.
   As Zeus lay resting, happy, satisfied;
   Sleep came on him, war's discord to hide.

150

Sleep descended earthwards, at the run,
To say that now the Greeks may briefly thrive;
Their famous tribes were roused by Poseidon,
He called on all, in mighty voice, to strive,
To beat back Hector from the narrow ships.
Because Achilles lingers in his pride,
He said: "Let urgent vows come from your lips,
Advance as one, let none your charge divide.
Pick up your shields and take your longest spears;
Prepare to fight against our deadly foe,
Let tired and wounded set aside their fears
And seize sharp bronze to lay the Trojans low."
      With his sword Poseidon took the lead,
      Its mighty blade on Greek blood keen to feed.

151

Troy also readied, though the weaker side,
Where, brilliant Hector, urged his legions on;
The armies closed then like the roaring tide,
Pushed landwards till the rolling dunes are won.
Dire war cries sounded fury, raging loud,
And as they charged the voice of terror rose.
First glorious Hector cast at Ajax, proud,
Yet sword and shield strap stopped his deadly blows.
Then, huge Ajax hurled back in reply
A mighty rock, which spun great Hector round.
He dropped his spear and all the Greeks let fly
In hope, with lance, that each may kill or wound.
      Then all Troy's bravest gathered with their shields
      To shelter Hector—none to Greek ire yields.

152

The Trojans carried Hector, groaning, back,
To whirling Xanthus' stream, to gain his breath;
His strength was broken by the Greek's attack,
Thus there he rested, hurt, yet safe from death.
The Argives, seeing him they feared, withdraw,
Regained their war-craft, rushing forth to kill;
There, the lesser Ajax at the fore
Killed most with speed of foot and deadly skill.
Flesh was spoiled by bronze, and bloody gore
Spilled out upon that plain, where dark death flew
To gather legions in its hungry maw.
Blood debts were paid; so many then were due.
      Thus entrails spilled out 'mid men's dying moans,
      For each one slain, another's death atones.

Book 15

153

The Trojan throng retreated past the ditch
And there, though terrified, they held their ground.
Then Zeus awoke from those deep slumbers which
Had blessed the Greeks with chance to rally round.
He looked on Hector lying on the plain,
Then turned on Hera with accusing words;
He vowed for treason he would bring down pain
On all of those who'd helped the Argive swords.
Hera, frightened, vowed by Earth and Styx
That she had never aided Poseidon,
He'd seen Danaans hard pressed by their ships
And vowed to aid them till their cause was won.
  Zeus smiled forgiveness, telling her to go
  To summon Iris there with Apollo.

154

Zeus told Hera what his will would be:
With noble deaths, and end of Ilion,
But not until that—'granted destiny',
Begged by Thetis, glorified her son.
Hera to Olympus, fast as thought,
Flew in fear, his orders to obey,
There she took a cup which Themis brought,
The gods then heard her speak with much dismay.
She told them to accept all evils sent
For Zeus was lord and master of them all.
Yet Ares raged and would not give consent
To forgo vengeance, locked in Zeus's thrall.
  He ordered Fear and Terror harnessed then,
  And armoured, to bring bitter death to men.

155

Athene then in fear for all the gods
Took off the helmet from red Ares' head,
And snatched his spear lest all should stand at odds
With Zeus, she pleaded: "Do what he has said!"
With violent Ares by her words restrained,
Iris and Apollo were sent forth
To do what their great leader had ordained,
And tell Poseidon of his brother's wrath.
Wind footed Iris swiftly sped to find
The sea god with the message sent from Zeus;
At first Poseidon, angered, would not bend,
To threats the aegis-bearer vowed to use.
   He said in rank were equal, brothers three
   Who ruled the dead, the sky, and vasty sea.

156

Iris sought to change the sea-god's heart,
Reminding him: the Furies would abide
And always with the elder, take his part,
If conflict now must Rhea's sons divide.
Though vexed, Poseidon knew he must give way,
He left the Argives—merging with the sea.
Then Zeus sent swift Apollo down to say,
To Hector, he must strive for victory.
As Troy's chief sat there, weakly, on the ground
Apollo breathed huge strength into his limbs
Then as some stallion, wild, with thunderous sounds
Revived, he rode to where war's minstrel sings.
   Phoebus Apollo, of the golden sword,
   Thus urged to horse the waiting Trojan horde.

157

Now, as huntsmen living in the wild,
Whose hounds have put to flight a hornéd stag,
The Argives stared at Hector, wits beguiled,
That he into a lion on some crag
Seemed changed—and turned pursuers to pursued.
There Thoas wondered that this thing could be,
With Hector risen from death's multitude,
By Zeus revived to fill his destiny.
Thoas then ordered champions to the van
While all the rest retreated to the ships;
The bravest then stepped forward as one man,
Each desperate hand his shield and long spear grips.
   Troy's wolves descended as one pack to feed
   With bronze on Argive flesh, with lusty greed.

158

Apollo, wearing mist about his form,
Held high the aegis bringing terror down.
Yet Argive courage held against Troy's storm
As arrows rained and deadly spears were thrown.
But as Apollo stared into their eyes
And shook the aegis, all their valour went;
They all flew back as sheep caught by surprise
By two wild beasts which prowled on slaughter bent.
Hector took first blood as was his due,
Polydamas, Aeneas brought down death,
Agenor and Paris forwards flew,
To steal Greek souls and rob their lungs of breath.
   Danaans, backwards blundered, through the ditch.
   Hector commanded: "Make straight for their ships!"

159

The Trojan crowd rolled on, whipped forth by words.
Apollo led the way and made a path,
Which bridged the ditch-way for the massing hordes
Who streamed across, new filled with warlike wrath.
They wrecked the bastions of the fleeing Greeks
As easily as sand walls on the shore
Are shattered by a small boy's careless feet,
To lie where splendid ramparts stood before.
The Argives reined in, standing by their ships,
And there out loud Geranian Nestor prayed,
To Zeus, to save them from that fear which grips
All fleeing legions, desperate, disarrayed.
      Zeus of the councils heard and thundered back,
      But this encouraged Troy in its attack.

160

The desperate Greeks climbed high upon the prows
Of their black ships and fought with long sea pikes.
While Eurypylus's skill endows
Patroclus, there, swift healing for his stripes.
That lord lamented then, when loud he heard
Harsh sounds of conflict rising from the wall;
He went in hope Achilles could be stirred
To action by the need to heed war's call.
Back at the ships, though both sides strained and tried
And many ended, neither army won.
Though mighty Ajax, Hector's charge denied
His strength could not Troy's warlord overcome.
      Then Caletor came forth with eyes of fire,
      The spear of Ajax sent him to death's pyre.

161

Hector saw his noble cousin die
And called on all, his body to defend.
Then with his lance at Ajax he let fly,
Yet brought the son of Mastor to his end.
Ajax shuddered, calling Teucer on,
To claim revenge there for their fallen friend;
The archer let his deadly arrows run
Amid the Trojans; life from flesh to rend.
A shaft for Hector then the bowman picked,
But Zeus, his guardian, broke the curved horn's twine,
The bow flew sideways as the arrow clipped
It from his hands, thus willed by one divine.
  Teucer cursed that gods should interfere,
  But Ajax ordered: "Take up now your spear.".

162

Ajax urged in frenzy—Greeks must fight!
Whilst Hector called for fury from the brave.
He raged to set the black ships all alight
With fires, from which, the Argives, none could save.
With strength and spirit stirred on either side
The legions rallied, killing one for one;
There many fell to wounds, while others died
As death by savage bronze from life was won.
Though Greeks defended, yet Troy's men advanced,
They came like lions ravening for food,
The Argives faltered as by fear entranced,
For Zeus drew courage from their paling blood.
  The son of Cronos honoured one that day
  A son of Priam, bright in war's array.

163

Zeus had promised Thetis, that her prayer
Would be accomplished and the day be won,
But not before proud Hector from his lair
Brought fire down to the ships, destroying one.
Thus he waited for that single flare
Which marked the apogee of Troy's attack.
Then Greeks would rise and Trojans, in despair,
Would by their fury then be driven back.
'Though Hector's life ran low, his glory now
Would be as great as Zeus gave any man,
And though he probed to reach the nearest prow,
None would yield to his destroying plan'.
      They closed about him then like mighty cliffs
      Which hold back seas which winter's tempest whips.

164

Yet Hector charged again as storm sired clouds,
Which strain the sails and bend the groaning mast,
Then hide the ship beneath sea-foaming shrouds
And fill the crew with fear brought on their blast.
Then like a lion, murderous, who falls
On cattle with his bloodied claws to feed;
He claimed one from Mycenae for death's halls,
Which let loose terror, 'mid Greek ranks to breed.
Their line retreated to the first ship's ends
And near defeat they all heard Nestor pray,
Reminding—each, his lands and kin defends;
That they must hold, for shame, to save the day.
      Whilst his brave words caused courage, fast, to grow
      Athene gave them light to see their foe.

165

A mighty sea-pike, Ajax took in hand
And with huge steps strode up and down the deck.
Though there the Argives held, at his command,
No spear of Greece could Hector's anger check.
There, as a flashing eagle in the plunge
On birds which swarm by river banks to feed;
No force may stop his wild and reckless lunge,
Where promise is fulfilled by sacred deed.
Now Hector took the prow and called for fire,
Whilst all around, they fought with sword and axe;
The earth ran black with blood from battle's ire
As then that day came close to its climax.
      Bright Hector urged all onwards to their prize,
      His men pressed harder at each trapped Argive.

166

Troy's volleys drove back Ajax from the prow,
To mid-ships, where he thought would follow—death,
There, standing firm with pike, he bellowed now
To all the Greeks to fight to their last breath.
He shouted: "That no others come in aid!
That no defences stand but spears and shields!
Now all must hold or evermore be paid
In that base coin which comes to him who yields."
He held his post with back against the sea
And called, "Salvation now lies in our hands."
With pike he warded of that victory
Which would have driven Greece from Troy's fair lands.
      Though twelve rushed forward, bearing burning brands,
      The same lay wounded on those blood soaked sands.

Book 16

167

Patroclus, to Achilles went and wept,
And told him of those grief's which fell upon
The Argives and that weapon's hail which swept
Upon their heroes, wounding every one.
He begged that great lord, as he would not fight
That all his Myrmidons should have release
To follow him, geared in that armour bright
Of great Achilles, bringing Greeks relief.
Danaans seeing this would courage gain,
Whilst all the clans of Troy would feel dismay;
To see Achilles from his truce abstain
And think he rushed back fiercely to the fray.
      In innocence, his supplications there
      Were soon the bitter fruits of death to bear.

168

Achilles thus reluctantly agreed
To let Patroclus put his armour on,
And then to lead his Myrmidons with speed
To fight Troy at the ships, till all were gone.
He placed a stern injunction on his friend,
That this deed done, he must at once return
And to the dry plains other Argives send,
And not in pride for battle honours yearn.
Back at the black ships Ajax could not hold
As evil volleys rained down where he stood;
Then gleaming Hector with his sword made bold
To cleave his spear-head from the strong ash wood.
      Ajax shuddered, turning fast away,
      Knowing where the will of Lord Zeus lay.

169

The Trojans brought down, weariless, red fire,
Then quenchless flame spread over all the ship.
Achilles as he saw that raging pyre
Told Patroclus—"Rapidly equip!"
His friend then took that god-wrought armour, bright,
And round his shins first placed the well wrought greaves,
With silver clasps they gripped his ankles tight,
The corselet next he took from Achilles—
Chased with stars, to decorate the breast,
He donned it, taking then his silvered sword
And heavy shield and helm with horsehair crest,
Whose plumes of terror marked its dreaded lord.
  And last two spears, yet not that mighty one
  Which Cheiron had brought down from Pelion.

170

Automedon, then went to yoke the steeds:
Immortals, gifted with the west wind's speed.
Achilles roused his men for deadly deeds
Those Myrmidons who aided him in need.
As wolves that tear flesh raw in ceaseless anger
With tireless fury, till jowls run with blood;
They armoured, ready then, for none may linger
When tides of war run wildly at the flood.
Men from fifty ships that lord commanded,
Of whom, Achilles picked out leaders, five;
Then at their stations, in stern words, demanded;
That there for deathless glory all should strive.
  Then on the ships his hungry pack descends,
  Those men with eyes of fire and hearts of fiends.

171

Achilles, troubled, to his shelter went
And found the chest which lovely Thetis gave;
Inside it was the goblet Zeus had sent,
Reserved for when libations must be made.
He scoured the vessel clean with sulphur stones
And washed it clean with water from the spring,
Then poured in wine and prayed in reverent tones
That Zeus should to Patroclus glory bring,
And lead him back to safety, fighting done.
Prayers were made: the son of Cronos heard him,
And of the two things asked for, granted one:
The life-light of Patroclus, soon must dim.
　　　Libations made, Achilles went to stand
　　　And watch his friend make combat, hand to hand.

172

The Myrmidons came streaming down like wasps
Made angry by the torments of young boys,
There each one in his soul wild fury clasps
As down around the ships, that swarm deploys.
Patroclus then called out so loud and clear:
"Remember now what we are sent to bring!
The greatest of the Argives sends us here,
The valour of his henchmen, measures him."
The Trojans there who saw the roaring throng,
Looked on that reckless charge with sheer dismay,
Shaken, that Achilles seemed to come,
Each looked around for paths to run away.
　　　For all then feared the death which winged toward
　　　Their legions, borne on axe and spear and sword.

173

The leader of those bold Paeonian lords
Pyraechmes was the first of all to die;
Patroclus thus drove fear among Troy's hordes,
Who then from half burnt ships in panic fly.
Danaans streamed back strong, as battle's clamour
Rose like thunder, stirred by Cronos' son;
Though Trojans tried against the Argive armour,
It was by Greek lords, deeds of death were done.
As wolves bring havoc to spring herds with fury,
When, then, the young ones fall to them as prey,
That panic ran among the Trojan army
As sheep which see their new-born snatched away.
        The valour which had driven Troy was gone,
        Then they remembered terror, every one.

174

In the mêlée, Ajax looked to slay
Hector, with a spear cast from his arm.
The Trojan with his shield would not give way
And used his war-craft well, avoiding harm.
With outcry they fell back in shamed retreat
Confusion's streams then ran across Troy's plain.
Patroclus urged on Argives to defeat
Those whom he saw yet by their ships remain.
His swift, immortal, horses swiftly drew
His car across that ditch, where many spilled;
Though to safety Hector's horses flew,
Their flight with that great lord occurred, unwilled.
        There dust clouds rose from feet which choked the ways,
        Of those who sought an exit from death's maze.

175

The noise which rose from Troy's steeds as they fled
Was as those waters on an autumn day
Which Zeus sends down in rage, and mortals dread,
When for impious actions they must pay.
Then all their rivers swell in fullest spate,
As through the dark ravines fast waters flee,
No works of man their forces can abate
As with huge roar they crash down to the sea.
Patroclus ran swift, slaying, through their ranks
Pronous there and Thestor he cut down;
And others at the centre and the flanks,
He reaped that harvest: death, which war had sown.
  It seemed that into rout Troy's day had run,
  Until into the fray came Sarpedon.

176

From their chariots leapt down those two
As hook clawed vultures screaming for revenge;
Then in wild frenzy, at each other flew
With bitter bronze, in deadliest exchange.
Zeus who watched them knew their destiny
And spoke to Hera, pitying, of one
Who fate had marked out for death's victory,
The dearest of all men, young Sarpedon.
He pondered, if to thwart, 'the writ of doom'
For he could lift the hero far away;
A thought condemned by other gods there, whom
Had sons who fought amid that deadly fray.
  Hera said to ease the pain of loss
  Send down to him lords Hypnos, Thanatos.

177

Zeus then knew he could not disobey
And yet wept tears of blood for his dear son
Who by fate's laws had come to his last day,
For him life's sands had little time to run.
Patroclus threw the first spear bringing death
To Thrasymelus, henchman to Troy's chief.
Then Sarpedon robbed Pedasus of breath
That mortal steed was sent where night holds fief.
Automedon slashed through the fouled trace rein
And once again the heroes thundered close,
Then Sarpedon a bronze spear cast in vain
And Patroclus his second lance let loose.
       This ran true and struck the beating heart
       Of Sarpedon, who there must life depart.

178

That lord fell as an oak or towering pine
Hewn down by axes whetted for the task,
He clawed the dust and roared in mortal pain
To Glaucus: "You must do the thing I ask!
Defend the body that this Greek has won."
Patroclus braced his heel against the chest
To drag his spearhead out from Sarpedon
And with it, life, the ruined body left.
Yet Glaucus could not aid his fallen friend
As pain still from his wound ran through his arm;
He prayed that lord Apollo swift might send,
Him strength to save the corpse from further harm.
       Apollo heard his prayer and stopped the pain,
       Then healed the wound so he might fight again.

179

Then Glaucus roused up all the Lycians
To fight to reclaim, fallen, Sarpedon
And drive away the wolfish Myrmidons;
Dishonour to his corpse, then could not come.
Whilst Hector lead in fury those from Troy,
Patroclus roused the Argives to defend,
So they could hold the body and destroy
Those who came to claim their fallen friend.
The Lycians and Myrmidons fought hard
And Trojans thrusted 'gainst Achaian shields,
And shouldered back the Greek ranks yard by yard,
Then came the turn of Ilium's men to yield.
> Glaucus then came forth, yet no side won,
> And weapons piling high hid Sarpedon.

180

The armies buzzed like flies around the corpse,
As those which swarm round milk pails in the spring.
Then Zeus glared downwards, giving angry thought
To how death's curse to Patroclus he'd bring.
It seemed that it would serve his purpose best
If all the Grecian forces made for Troy;
He stole away the strength from Hector's breast,
Who thus called out to all around to fly.
They stripped the armour then from Sarpedon
And to the ships they bore it as their prize.
Zeus then sent swift Apollo to his son
To save him from the gore of his demise.
> The corpse he washed and carried far away
> There, honoured, in ambrosial robes it lay.

181

Then, in charge of those twins: Death and Sleep,
The silent form of Sarpedon was placed,
To take for green Lycia's groves to keep;
Forever honoured, nevermore disgraced.
Patroclus charged then at the Trojan horde
For, raw blind fury spurred him to his fate;
'Forgo this', was the last commanding word
By which Achilles tried to curb his hate.
But there besotted by his bloodlust's urge
Patroclus reached the towers at Troy's gate.
There, thrice, Apollo stopped his fury's surge
He came again, then darkly, Phoebus spoke.
      Give way, for Troy will never fall to you
      Nor to Achilles is that glory due.

182

Avoiding danger, Patroclus gave way,
To him whose anger brings death from afar.
Behind Troy's gates, in safety, Hector lay,
And pondered if he should charge out to war.
Apollo in disguise as Asius,
Described his path to glory, if he went
And gained by arms the death of Patroclus;
Thus back to fight, in hope, was Hector sent.
Patroclus saw him springing, swift, to ground,
And took a jagged stone up which he threw
It missed great Hector, yet another found
That deadly mass at Cebriones flew.
      Thus Hector's driver's skull, by it was smashed,
      There falling down to earth he breathed his last.

Hermes directs Hypnos and Thanatos as they lift the body of Sarpedon.

183

Patroclus mocked: "How agile was that fall,
Like one who dives for oysters from a boat,"
And then above the body he stood tall,
Till Hector sprang to spoil the Argive rout.
They fought like lions over a killed deer
With raging hunger, each to claim the prize,
At head and foot they at the body tore
Yet matched in strength, each, victory denies.
Their armies clashed as east and southern winds
Which in the valleys shake the crowded trees.
There volleys, thick, from those opposing bands
Sent many to their final destinies.
      As evening came Achaian might grew strong,
      And from death's clamour Cebriones won.

184

Patroclus charged the Trojan legions thrice,
Each time he came he cut down foemen: nine;
Yet on the fourth, Apollo by device,
Well veiled in mist slipped through the battle line,
And struck that hero, casting down his helm,
He stood defenceless, dizzy, with wits dimmed;
Euphorbus speared him, opening death's realm,
Which he must enter as Lord Zeus had deemed.
Hector saw Patroclus try to fly,
And drove his spear point through his midriff clear;
Then all, in horror, saw that he must die,
The one, whom to Achilles was most dear.
      Thunderously then, Patroclus fell,
      The Argive groans there tolled his dying knell.

185

Hector stood above the fallen one
And spoke in triumph then, with wingéd words;
That though for Troy's destruction he had come,
Soon, he would be carrion for birds.
Replied Patroclus, "Though my death is yours,
But for Apollo, this would not be so;
Twenty like you with their shining spears
Without his help could not have laid me low.
That god's help, with Euphorbus' spear, combined
To cloud my strength with deadly destiny.
You take my life now as great Zeus has deigned,
Poor, third slayer, in this victory."
      With dying words he spoke this prophecy:
      "That soon in Hades you will sleep, near me."

Book 17

186

Menelaus saw Patroclus fall
And quickly ran, his body to bestride;
There with spear and shield he threatened all;
Those who came to claim him, he denied.
Euphorbus ran to face him boasting how
He was first to spear the lordly Greek.
He said: "Stand back, give me his body now
For you must taste that bitter thing, defeat."
Menelaus, angry at those taunts,
Spoke to Zeus of those who vaunt their pride,
And said: "Death often comes to him who flaunts
His warlike skill, as one by fate denied."
      He warned Euphorbus—"Flee back to the throng;
      For if you stay, your life will not be long."

187

Euphorbus though was stayed by his blood feud,
To claim revenge there for a brother killed;
He came to slay, his spear with death imbrued
Was then in hate at his opponent willed.
Its point though bent back on the sturdy shield
Of the Greek, who lunged and caught him true,
He fell, pierced through the neck upon the field;
There laid with blood smeared locks, his end he knew.
Though nurtured as an olive tree full grown,
War's raging tempest wrenched him to the ground;
Then Menelaus faced all Trojans down,
Until Apollo, valiant Hector found.
      Then stirred to anger by that sight he saw,
      With piercing scream he ran back into war.

188

Menelaus, hearing that shrill cry,
Stood deeply troubled, speaking to his heart.
Should he stand alone, his spear to try,
Or leave Achilles armour and depart?
Led by Hector all of Troy came on
And though reluctant Sparta's king gave ground;
He looked around for Telamon's great son
And soon amid the mass, that war-chief found.
He begged the mighty one, without delay,
To come with him the fallen one to save;
Patroclus, there, without his armour lay,
Where Trojans could defile him like a slave.
      And give him to the waiting dogs of Troy,
      Unless Greek spears could vengeful plans destroy.

189

Ajax charged and Hector turned away,
Yet bore the god wrought armour from the field.
Then holding all the Trojan lords at bay,
Astride Patroclus, Ajax would not yield.
With Menelaus standing by his side
They seemed to put great Hector's flight to shame
And Glaucus, darkly, blamed him in his pride
For running from those Greeks of valiant name.
Reproving, Hector made his purpose clear,
And told all—"Fight now, whilst I quickly don
The armour of Achilles, bought so dear
From him who slew my guest-friend: Sarpedon."
      Thoughts of death then darkened Zeus' strong brow,
      Yet he gave Hector strength to fight, for now.

190

Ares gifted Hector all his might
And Priam's son then fell upon the Greeks.
He ranged through Troy's ranks urging all to fight
And promised gifts to him who glory seeks,
By seizing dead Patroclus back again.
That man would have a half of all the spoils
And share with Hector equally the fame;
Thus, all charged, hopeful, back amid war's toils.
Great Telamonian Ajax stood there, grim,
And tore the life from those who ventured near;
He gave up hope for self and Sparta's king
As from war's cloud he felt death must appear.
  He asked brave Menelaus then to call
  His great war-cry out loud, to rally all.

191

Then all rushed forward, valiant, lest in shame
Patroclus should be taken for Troy's dogs.
Ajax son of Oileus, first came
Then Meriones—Idomeneus.
These, the valiant vanguard, firmly stood
Against the raging flood tide loosed by Troy;
Thus those who come must pay the price in blood,
If fallen Patroclus they would destroy.
At first that torrent pushed the Greek lords back
And Troy's wild hordes, his bloodied body claimed,
But Ajax wheeled and ran to the attack
And with his strength the fallen one, regained.
  Thus with a wild boar's might, in savage pride,
  That noble corpse to Trojan hands denied.

192

With Ajax there, and Hector to the fore,
Men from both sides fell in that mêlée;
The Trojans took their comrades from the war,
As Argive might raged forwards, they gave way.
Apollo stirred Aeneas in the form
Of Periphas, the herald, still to try,
He gave him hope that victory could come;
The Trojan lord could not the god deny.
He leapt before the rest with spear to kill
And took down Leocritus, but his friend,
Lycomedes, returned the thrust to still
Apisaon, who fell, to meet his end.
      And though the Trojans drove to gain the corpse,
      The Argives ringed Patroclus with their force.

193

Gigantic Ajax made his men hold close
And from their bronze the ground ran red with blood.
Though many Greeks died, Troy's ranks lost the most
As Argive beat back death where comrade stood.
The Greeks fought on, unwearying, like fire,
The bravest of them all in shrouding mist,
Whilst on the spacious plain the rest aspired
To distant combat, where spears flew—and missed.
Yet in the centre bitter battle raged
As both sides struggled for the fallen one.
Far off, Achilles thought Patroclus lived
And Thetis hid from him the evil done.
      The Argives swore that they must hold or die
      In glory there, with Patroclus to lie.

194

Some Trojans, filled with war thoughts, also vowed
That they must stay, not thinking to give way,
And each from each called forth the spirit proud
In hope Dardanian fire might win the day.
In iron hard tumult, 'neath a brazen sky,
The sounds of conflict filled the barren air;
The horses of Achilles stood nearby
And wept tears for their driver, in despair.
The son of Cronos pitied as they grieved,
And wondered why as gifts to dismal man,
Those two immortals from the gods were cleaved,
To learn to mourn for those of life's short span.
  Thus, new vigour into both he breathed,
  To save their master with their whirlwind speed.

195

Automedon then charged the Trojan mass;
War's chariot bore him lightly, but alone,
And thus his thirsting spear he could not cast,
Until Alcimedon saw what was done
And vaulted in the car to take the reins;
Automedon, thus freed, sprang down to fight,
Yet Hector had observed those drivers change,
And thought that now those wind-hoofed horses might
At last be taken as his well-earned prize.
He called on lord Aeneas to attend
And both went forward sheltered by shield hides.
Automedon, those steeds must now defend.
  He called on those most valiant Greeks to come,
  To check the dreaded charge of Priam's son.

196

Automedon then cast his deadly spear
And pierced the shield of hopeful Aretus;
Who there gained death and not the sought for gear,
And paid in part for lordly Patroclus.
Automedon, avoided Hector's lance,
Which winged towards him searching for revenge,
With thirsting swords the two made their advance
But both Aiantes stepped forth to challenge
The coming Trojans, who in fear gave ground.
The Grecian lord then stripped the spoils of war
From Aretus, while blood poured from his wound,
Then laid them safe and mounted his swift car.
      Athene, next came there, with hope to stir
      Danaan courage; lifting black despair.

197

The goddess in the form of Phoinix spoke
To Menelaus, saying—now comes shame!
If Patroclus by spear or bronze sword stroke
Is mutilated on this blood soaked plain.
He answered then his father, unaware
That in his guise appeared the owl-eyed one.
Athene, happy, answered his strong prayer
And filled with daring Atreus's son.
Astride Patroclus there, he killed Podes,
A friend who mighty Hector greatly prized.
Apollo scolded, "See that great king dares
To stand alone, and all of Troy defies."
      The shroud of sorrow then was Hector's spur
      As god loosed fear and thunder fill the air.

198

'Mid thunder's crash then Greeks retreat, in fear,
And wounded men draw back with spirit gone.
At Hector, Idomeneus cast a spear,
Which shattered on his breast as he came on.
Hector threw and struck the charioteer
Of Meriones, piercing jaw and tongue.
He dropped his reins as Troy's hordes, fast, came near
And fell to earth; his worldly work was done.
Yet Meriones caught the reins and called,
To Idomeneus, to mount and flee;
He saw that now the Grecian charge had stalled
And Zeus once more lured Troy to victory.
      Ajax then despaired at what he saw,
      And called for council on the needs of war.

199

It seemed that Hector's fury now would win
That body, which the Greeks sought to defend;
Then Ajax thought, amid the battle's din,
To tell Achilles of his fallen friend.
He sought a runner but the swirling mist
Hid the Argives, thus great Ajax prayed
That Zeus would now this cloaking darkness lift,
In answer then, with light, the hot sun blazed.
Then Ajax called to Menelaus—"Seek
Antilochus, great hearted Nestor's son,
For, if alive, this news of which we speak
He must convey about the fallen one."
      Menelaus thus heard and then obeyed
      And left Patroclus, 'mid that mêlée laid.

200

As Menelaus went off, those left behind,
He urged with greater efforts to defend
Patroclus, who in life to all was kind,
While he looked out for Nestor's son to send
To lord Achilles, swiftly; if he lived.
Then like an eagle, turning everywhere,
With piercing eyes those swarming ranks he sieved
And on the left, Antilochus, found there.
He told him of the death of Patroclus,
And sent him to Achilles with the word,
Of sorrow, which described the awful loss;
In tears he sped to find the mighty lord.
   With message sent, all thought he would not come
   For who could fight, when armour he had none.

201

All took council, how best to survive,
Yet save the corpse from that wild Trojan band.
Ajax said to Meriones: "Strive:
To stoop and lift Patroclus from the ground,
And carry him to safety while we hold
These Dardanians, ravening for blood."
They saw the body shouldered by the bold
Lord Meriones, where great Ajax stood,
And with a roar rushed forward like wild hounds
Who scenting blood, would take a wounded boar;
Those dogs came onwards, then with painful wounds
Retired as the Aiantes taught them war.
   Hard back, the Trojans stand as craven curs
   With cheeks turned pale by fear, which at them gnawed.

202

Thus the corpse of Patroclus was saved
And carried back near to the hollow ships;
Whilst 'mid that struggle both Aiantes braved
Troy's tide, which like the ocean forward rips.
There standing as a timbered ridge they hold,
Like that which keeps back waters on the plain,
No breach was made beyond those standing, bold,
Although the Trojans came, again, again.
The young Achaians flocked like screaming birds
And fled in terror seeing Hector come,
With lord Aeneas, both with deadly swords,
Then ran to safety, joy in battle gone.
      On both sides of the ditch fine armour lay
      As fighting surged unchecked throughout that day.

Book 18

203

The messenger, Antilochus, came fast
And found Achilles, sat beside the ships;
That great heart then, his troubled spirit asked,
What sorrows now the gods upon him wished.
Nestor's son approached and wept warm tears,
And told him of the fate of Patroclus.
Thus hearing that the worst of all his fears
Had come to pass, he fouled his face with dust
And tore his hair while lying on the ground.
Then all his captive maidens ran to mourn
And beat their breasts with cries, and ran around,
Till fainting near Achilles prostrate form.
  In fear that grief should make him seek his end,
  Antilochus restrained his mourning friend.

204

Achilles cried so loud that in the deeps
His lady mother, Thetis, heard the sound.
Then her shrill wail through all the sea's depths sweeps,
To call the Nereids to gather round.
In sorrow then she led a threnody,
Its mourning echoes filled her silvery cave,
She told her sisters of that destiny:
Of death, which fate to great Achilles gave.
Lamenting, that he never would come home
She left to find him on the Trojan shore;
She found him there, sad, sighing and alone
And asked him of the suffering he bore.
  He told her of his dear companion's loss
  And promised vengeance there for Patroclus.

205

Weeping Thetis told him that his death
Must follow Hector's, due to fate's decree.
Thus knowing soon must come his final breath
He answered—he must meet his destiny
Whenever Zeus decreed that it must come;
Yet now he would win glory in the war.
Then Thetis pleaded with her godlike son;
Until she brought him armour back once more
From lord Hephaestus at tomorrow's dawn,
To hold back from his waiting destiny.
Then, to tell their father where she'd gone
She sent the Nereids beneath the sea.
   She hoped once more the mighty smith would make
   Glorious armour, for her dear son's sake.

206

All the while the war raged on the plain
Around the fallen form of Patroclus;
Hector fought in fury like a flame,
Whilst missiles fell like rain around the corpse.
Three times he seized its heels and pulled away;
Three times the strong Aiantes drove him back,
Yet Hector's rage would then have won the day
For no Greek there could hold his wild attack.
Hera sent winged footed Ira now
To rouse Achilles, once again to fight;
He told her then of Thetis and his vow,
That he could not, until the dawn's first light.
   Thus lacking armour nothing could be done
   For now he thought, to save Menoetius' son.

207

The goddess told him: merely let them see
You stand in anger high above the wall,
And Troy, in terror, then must turn and flee,
If they think you've answered battle's call.
Athene swept the Aegis round him then
And wrapped his form around with golden flame,
He went and stood apart from other men
So all could see that once again he came.
He stood and shouted with a brazen cry
Which drove down endless fear on Trojans there;
All hearts were shaken, then they turned to fly,
In rout, as thrice his great voice filled the air.
      Confusion reigned and twelve of Troy's best died
      By their own spears as from that fight they hied.

208

Patroclus, thus was saved and on a bier,
Was placed whilst all around his dear friends stood
In mourning there, Achilles too came near
And let warm tears about his dead friend flood.
Then Hera drove the sun god down to sink
Into the Ocean's depths and thus came night,
And now in council fearful Trojans think
On what to do before the dawn's first light.
For lord Achilles once more had appeared;
Polydamus described that sight with dread,
Advising all: avoid the one they feared
And take the path which to the city led.
      If any met Achilles on the plain
      He feared that there, as corpses, they'd remain.

209

Then looking at him darkly, Hector spoke,
And urged the Trojans all to stay and fight,
And don once more their armour and war's yoke
To face the Greeks and not give way to flight.
Then if Achilles came to try his skill
He would meet him; one of them would fall,
Great glory gained thus by the war-god's will,
By he who triumphed, standing, risking all.
The Trojans roared approval—those poor fools;
Athene there had clouded all their wits.
Thus Hector's black hate, wisdom overrules.
Then he made camp close to the narrow ships.
  Meanwhile, all through the night was mourned the loss,
  By Argive lords, of their friend Patroclus.

210

Achilles led the throng in chants of pain
And laid his hands upon his slaughtered friend.
They mourned all night, lamenting that his fame
By fates decree had found, in death, its end.
Then groaning like some lion who had found
His cubs were stolen when returning home,
He spoke to all the Myrmidons around
Of that vengeance which so soon would come.
He promised Hector's head and twelve from Troy,
In hate beheaded, stood before the pyre.
Death's preparations now had banished joy,
With water for them heated on the fire.
  For the body must of gore be cleansed,
  Then be with oil anointed, by his friends.

211

Thetis came to where Hephaestus worked
And Caris caught her hand and greeted her,
And bade her sit and entertainment brought,
Then called her husband to the silver chair.
He there recalled his rescue from that fall,
When cast out by his mother, being lame;
Of Thetis and his labours in her thrall,
For nine years hid from Hera and her shame.
He set aside his bellows and his tools
And washed his massive neck and hairy chest,
Then with those servants' which his cunning rules,
He went to ask then how to serve her best.
　　　She spoke about those sorrows in her heart
　　　And begged him forge new armour with his art.

212

Hephaestus promised that he would create
Such armour as no mortal ever saw;
He ordered thus his bellows, fire to wake,
With flames blown high, renewed in throaty roar.
Then first with all his skill he forged a shield
With triple rim and five fold in array;
He, with his cunning on the first revealed:
The heavens and glorious sun which rules the day.
The Pleiades and Hyades and Bear,
Which looks towards Orion as it turns,
Alone it never enters Ocean's lair
As all those other shapes which mind discerns.
　　　And on the second segment then he forged
　　　Affairs of men, of peace and of discord.

213

He wrought two cities there, of war and peace,
With marriages in one and festivals,
With brides by torchlight led unto the feast,
Where flutes and lyres made merry those revels.
Yet in the market place a dispute raged,
And elders sat and listened to decide
On how the asked for blood price should be paid,
In restitution for a man who'd died.
There, heralds held the people back with staves
And both men pleaded hotly in debate,
And on the ground were two gold pieces laid;
A prize for he who best could arbitrate.
      Outside the second city armies lay,
      While those inside held firm those troops at bay.

214

Whilst aged men and boys, the ramparts held,
The rest prepared an ambush for the foe,
And by the river's bank, two shepherds killed,
Who'd brought the army's herd to water, slow.
Then, in the frozen bronze, pursuit was seen,
With war's confusion found amid cast spears,
And all the hate destructive death could glean
Was ever etched on faces, with their fears.
A fertile field he made, wide, triple ploughed,
With oxen turning when they reached its end,
With honeyed wine as rich reward allowed,
For ploughmen as they found each waiting bend.
      Behind their blades it seemed the gold turned dark
      Like earth, new furrowed by the ploughman's work.

215

He turned, to forge the precinct of a king,
With peasants reaping and cut swathes of corn,
And binders tying with the cords they bring,
While children gathered through the golden morn.
The king in silence, happy, watched them all,
While heralds made a feast beneath a tree;
A roasting ox there, waited supper's call
And round it women scattered white barley.
In gold and silver, he, a vineyard wrought,
With field-ditch gouged out and a fence of tin,
A single path, to it, grape pickers brought,
And to the lyre they gathered clusters in.
     A youth, the mourning songs of Linus sang,
     Thus through the vineyard airs of beauty rang.

216

He made horned oxen then of tin and gold,
Which thronged at speed from farm to pasturing.
Out by a reed bed where the river rolled,
Stood four herdsmen, with nine dogs attending.
Yet out in front two lions caught a bull,
Which, bellowing in pain, was dragged away.
The men urged on their dogs to hunt and kill,
But fear or prudent mind, held them at bay.
The strong armed smith forged vale and large meadow
With flocks and sheepfolds near a dancing floor,
Like Daedalus at Cnossus long ago,
Which lovely Ariadne oversaw.
     There built, elaborately, so her feet
     Could fly, entranced, to lute and tabor's beat.

217

On the floor danced young men and young girls,
Sought for their beauty, bought by oxen gifts,
There held, in youth's forever wistful whirls,
Fine garlanded, with hands gripped at the wrists.
The young men wore gold knives on silver belts,
And lightly ran in rows which crossed and flowed
In measured dance as summer's music lilts,
And all around them stood the happy crowd.
With Oceanus round the outer rim,
The shield was finished, thus with all complete:
Helm and corslet, greaves bright wrought from tin,
He laid it at Achilles' mother's feet.

   She took the shining gifts from Hephaestus
   And swept down like a hawk from Olympus.

Book 19

218

As dawn, in yellow robes, then gently rose
To carry her soft light to gods and men,
Thetis found her son with all of those
Who'd mourned with him, through all the long night then.
Before her weeping son she laid the gift
Of armour, which from heaven's skilled smith she bore.
The Myrmidons, in terror, would not lift
Their eyes to look upon it on the floor.
Only Achilles looked and anger came,
And caused his eyes to glitter, sharp with hate;
Now his tears and all his mourning pain
Called down revenge, which only death could sate.
     He asked his mother as he went to arm
     To save his dear friend's corpse from further harm.

219

Thus with ambrosia sweet and nectar red
Patroclus' corpse, with skill and care, she filled;
With danger of corruption from it fled
Achilles armoured as his mother willed,
And, brilliant, strode along the bloody shore,
Crying loud that all the Greeks should come
To meet and then prepare for deadly war;
In eager hope, assembled every one.
Achilles and great Agamemnon swore
To put their grievous quarrel far aside
And lay its blame at false Delusion's door,
Its crafty lures had filled them both with pride.
     For all who'd fallen at their hate's expense,
     Their unity would gain Greeks recompense.

220

Achilles hungered for the new attack,
Yet he of many talents gave advice:
That all should feast and for the while hold back;
Unfed and tired, his Greeks would pay the price
Impatience levied on those haste would lead,
For strength would fade as longer grew the day.
They did as great Odysseus had said
And ate and rested ready for the fray.
The lord of men was bade to bring those gifts
He'd promised and before them all to vow,
That he had never laid with fair Briseis
And that she was returned, unsullied, now.
      Great Agamemnon swore by gods and men—
      Brought gracious gifts to end their long feud then.

221

Agamemnon sent Laertes' son
To bring those gifts and dedicate a boar,
So Helios and Zeus would then be won
To their just cause and make them great in war.
In pain Achilles hungered for the fray;
Food and drink meant nothing to his heart,
He longed for slaughter all through night and day,
To bring death to the Trojans with his art.
Then spoke again Odysseus, the wise,
To tell him how the tides of battle turn:
"He risks defeat who sustenance denies,
Thus hold till day no matter how you yearn.
      With strength revived, relentless, all may go
      In deathless bronze, to war against the foe."

222

With his men Odysseus went to bring
The gifts from Agamemnon's hoarded store;
With tripods, cauldrons, horses from the king,
Ten talents of pure gold and furthermore—
Seven maids and with them, eighth, Briseis fair,
Talthybius then took out his knife,
And Agamemnon prayed and truly swore
By all the gods who rule on death and life
That fair Briseis remained untouched and pure.
Then with the bronze was cut the great boar's throat
And lifted high and whirled upon the shore
Then cast upon the sea, which stretched far out.
   Achilles said that Zeus had willed it all
   And now they must prepare for battle's call.

223

The council broke and all retired to dine:
The Myrmidons disposing of the gifts.
Briseis, dressed as love's goddess, divine,
Cried out in pain and tore her throat and breasts,
In sorrow, seeing Patroclus laid low.
She thought of all his kindness, 'mid the deaths,
Of her dear spouse and brothers and the vow
Of marriage to Achilles from his lips.
She spoke in lamentation filled with grief;
Her women round her with Briseis wept.
Achaia's lords urged that Achilles eat
But he abstained and sorrow's vigil kept.
   The anguish in him now would have no pause,
   Until, with death, he entered danger's jaws.

224

Remembrance filled the heart for his dear friend
And thoughts of home, fair Scyrus, and his son.
His hopes of a return were at an end
To Phthia, to show him trophies won.
He wondered if his father heart was stilled
Or sorrowed, waiting news of his son's death.
Then mourning thoughts, with gloom, the elders filled
As they recalled their homes and what they'd left.
In pity, Zeus then bade Athene go
And fill Achilles with red nectar sweet,
And with Ambrosia cause new strength to flow
Through limbs which fasting's curse was making weak.
      With god sent food she swooped down through the sky,
      To ease those pangs which victory deny.

225

Now, from the ships, they scattered like the snow
As driving flurries which on storm winds ride,
With corslets strong and ash spears in a row
And helmets shining bright with new found pride.
Earth seemed to laugh as massed feet thundered on,
The glare of gleaming bronze swept to the sky;
Before them, armoured, Peleus's son,
Whose eyes glowed fierce with fires of destiny.
With raging heart he donned those godly gifts
Which strong Hephaestus wrought with such great toil,
That armour, to his form perfectly fits—
Well armed, his psyche longed for war's turmoil.
      His shield gleamed as a fire which burns by night,
      To lead lost seamen by its mountain light.

226

Achilles then put on his mighty helm,
With horse-hair crest and edges chased with gold,
It shone out like a star in heaven's dark realm;
Though tight and close bronze sheets his limbs enfold,
Within the armour, bird-like, he moved free.
He then took down his father's Pelian spear
Which no one else could lift or use but he;
That mighty brand, which filled all Troy with fear.
His horses, those immortals, Balius
And Xanthus in their traces were prepared
To pull the war car of Achilleus,
Then these orders, dark, his swift steeds heard:
  "Podarge's children, listen every one,
  Be sure to bring me home when battle's done."

227

Xanthus bowed his head and answered him,
For lady Hera gave to him a voice,
"We will bring you safe back to your kin;
The gods decree it, we have little choice;
Yet soon your death will come, its day is sure,
The fates ordain what destiny must claim,
Their will and laws must endlessly endure;
Patroclus fell, a pawn in their vast game.
Though we run gifted with the West Wind's speed,
The fates spin out and cut the thread of life;
We may not change the span which they've decreed,
Its end comes when Atropos wields the knife."
  Achilles though disturbed to hear again
  That prophecy, must till then his vengeance claim.

Book 20

228

Insatiate of battle, Greeks prepared,
While on the plain all Trojans armoured too,
And from Olympus mighty Zeus declared
That all the gods must come to rendezvous.
Themis bore his message far and wide;
All river gods and nymphs of grove and spring
Swift came to listen at their father's side,
Apart from Ocean, who he could not bring.
Poseidon asked then, why was council called
While battle's embers almost burst to flame?
Zeus said: his summons many deaths forestalled,
And told them on Olympus he'd remain.
      Yet all the rest must help as was their will;
      Achilles thus would not, unhindered, kill.

229

For if the son of Peleus was seen
The Trojan legions then would, quick, retreat;
Achilles, thus, against great heaven's scheme
Would storm their walls and Zeus' high plans, defeat.
The gods went down with purposes opposed,
Poseidon, Hera and Athene went
With Hermes and Hephaestus to the Greeks.
Ares, Artemis and Leto leant
Support to Troy, which Hector's glory seeks.
Apollo, Aphrodite went with these.
That fear which fell when Troy saw Achilles
Was lifted, hope replacing dark despair.
      Both sides clashed as thunder crashed around
      And great Poseidon shook the battle ground.

230

Aidoneus, lord of the Shades below,
Sprang from his throne and screamed aloud in fear,
Poseidon might then rend the earth and so
The houses of the dead could then appear;
Revealing, ghastly, mouldering remains,
So that the very gods would shudder then,
But these were busy standing on Troy's plains
Each took his place among his chosen men.
Against Poseidon, Phoebus took his stand,
Athene stood against Enyalios
Hera's foe was Artemis whose hand
Brings death to all who soon her path must cross.
      Her mother, Leto, faced strong Hermes there
      And Xanthus must against Hephaestus dare.

231

Amid the mortals now proud spirits raged,
And lord Achilles strained and longed for war;
He knew by blood his grief would be assuaged
And could not rest till Hector's death was sure.
Apollo urged Aeneas at him first,
Appearing at his side as Lycaon
And gave him strength to try to lift Troy's curse
By bringing death to Peleus's son.
Yet Hera, of the white arms, saw him go
And knew by godly schemes he was inspired;
She bound the great immortals with a vow,
To save Achilles from that end desired.
      Poseidon, though, told all to watch and wait
      And let each man, unaided, meet his fate.

232

The gods retired to where great Heracles
Escaped the sea-beast, in his high built keep.
There, cloaked in cloud, they pondered ill at ease,
For all knew death soon many souls would reap.
The plain was filled with noise as pounding feet
Drummed on the earth below, which sagged and bowed;
Then from the throng two champions rushed to meet,
Before all others in that heaving crowd.
Aeneas first stood forth; his heavy helm
Moved with menace as he tossed his head.
He shook both spears and ran to overwhelm
Achilles, who came forward cloaked in dread.
     A baleful lion, straining there at bay
     Roused to fury, rushing to the fray.

233

As they came close Achilles, darkly, asked:
If Aeneas hoped to gain reward.
He said: "You come to find your death unmasked,
Look in my eyes and fear will dull your sword.
We met before in war, but for the gods,
I would have cut you down then in that chase;
They will not save you now for all the odds
Lie in my favour, death stares from my face."
He urged Aeneas, "Fly back in the ranks
To save your flesh from Hades' vasty halls."
In reply he said, "No Trojan slinks
From words, for none are deaf when battle calls.
     For through Anchises I descend from Zeus,
     My line of blood endures no pale excuse."

234

Thus finally he said: "Our words must end.
In this forward clearing we must fight,
I will not turn and now you must defend
Against my bronze, which brings you endless night."
Aeneas drove his pike against the shield
Which moaned as its wrought sheets, held point away.
Achilles feared the god made layers might yield
But only two of five of them gave way.
He then let fly the mighty Pelian ash
Which crashed right through the shield; yet at its rim,
Where bronze and hide were thinnest and no match
For that great brand, thrown with death's wings, by him.
     Aeneas shrank in fear far from the sound
     Of bronze on bronze upon that battle-ground.

235

Achilles drew his sharp edged sword and cried,
In baleful fury, sweeping to attack,
Aeneas seized a huge stone to decide
Their mortal struggle; neither may turn back.
Poseidon knew the Trojan prince must fall
And pleaded with the gods to intervene;
He knew that fate must on those lost heirs call,
That he must live, to sire Troy's new demesne.
Thus with mist he dulled Achilles' eyes
And pulled the great spear from Aeneas' shield,
And bore him from the field, and his demise,
And told him fate demanded he should yield.
     The mist dissolved, Achilles looked around,
     His spear, alone, lay on the silent ground.

236

He knew then that the gods had been at work
And urged his troops to answer battle's call;
He told the Argives none could duty shirk,
That he through Troy's massed ranks would lead them all.
But glorious Hector called to all his men
That they should stand and he would face alone
The dreaded one, who came in fury then;
Thus all Troy raised its spears to guard their home.
Apollo told great Hector then to wait
And meet Achilles in the multitude,
Into the swarm he darted fearing fate,
For now his foe came on, with hate imbrued.
  He slew Iphition, then running on
  Stabbed through the temple, brave Demoleon.

237

Hippodamas was speared and like a bull
He bellowed, dying, as his life poured out.
Achilles caught Polydorus right full
With lance thrown as he ran, the fray to scout.
For Priam would not let his youngest fight,
But from his navel now, the spear emerged.
He moaned and round him gathered mists of night
Then dropped as all of life from him was purged.
When Hector saw his brother's agony
He turned and went to face death's mighty lord
And raised his spear in hope of victory;
Achilles saw and gave him warning word:
  "That this approach for sure, ensures your end,
  In payment for the death of my dear friend."

238

Fearless Hector said that well he knew
That he was weaker and Achilles great,
And yet the gods brought death to one of two,
Thus the stronger then might meet his fate.
Balancing his spear he let it fly,
But great Athene blew the lance aside
And though Achilles came with vengeful cry,
Apollo wove a cloying mist to hide
Hector from his deadly bronze crowned spear.
Three times he charged and three times stabbed the air
He called out: "Dog the evil has come near,
The god has saved you, live and yet despair
     For I will win you at some later time,
     I also have the aid of those divine."

239

Achilles then advanced and killed Dryops,
Then with spear and sword felled Demouchus.
The sons of Bias there his fury drops;
He felled Laugonus then, and Dardanus.
Tros begged for mercy, yet he too was killed,
His liver pierced, his tunic drank black blood,
And many others as Achilles willed
Were sent to Hades, deadly was his mood.
It swept red fury as inhuman fire
Through all Troy's ranks, invincible he came,
His horses trampled all and his desire
For death remained unquenched or stayed by shame.
     With gore of battle on his bloody hands
     The lords of night were slaves to his commands.

Book 21

240

The Trojans came where whirling Xanthus streamed,
With dark Achilles riding in pursuit.
Then, half ran, where the walls of Troy safe gleamed
But half must try that raging river's route.
Like locusts pushed by fire they tumbled in,
Though jostled hard, they fought the eddied flow;
Banks echoed with their crying, and the din
Rose higher as Achilles laid them low.
For to the bank there strode that mighty lord,
His spear left leaning on the tamarisk,
He leapt into those currents with his sword,
To bring death like some awful basilisk.
  He struck around him with his deadly blade
  And none from Troy could then their fate evade.

241

The swirling currents of the stream grew red
With blood drawn from that fountain, born of Troy.
Achilles chose twelve living from the dead
To sacrifice and on his pyre destroy,
In vengeance for the death of Patroclus.
Into the crimson waters he returned
To fill with dread the channel of that fosse.
He there, Lycaon, Priam's son, discerned,
Who once was taken by him as a slave,
But ransomed recently he had returned
To Troy, and in that conflict win his grave;
For in Achilles heart great hatred burned.
  No words nor ransom there could win release,
  Revenge's ears are deaf to pity's pleas.

242

Before Achilles knelt poor Lycaon
To beg the right of ransom once again.
Without compassion spoke the mighty son
Of Peleus, of his revenge and pain.
He said: "My anger now descends on Troy,
Before Patroclus died such pleas might move
My mind to mercy, now death brings me joy,
As filled with hate my deadly sword will prove."
He slew Lycaon and the black blood flowed,
Achilles threw him then with cool disdain
Into the waters, calling out aloud:
"Lie with the fish, in their dark realm remain.
     There, dishonoured, let them strip your bones,
     To then be scattered where the rip-tide foams."

243

Achilles promised death would come to all
In payment for the slaughter of his friend;
And those Achaians answering war's call,
Who'd died, attempting their ships to defend.
Then anger rose, new, in the river's heart
As then he pondered how he best might save
Those men of Troy, whose time of life grew short,
As lord Achilles filled that flowing grave.
Now forwards ran the son of Pelegon,
For Xanthus filled his soul with valour's rage,
As of that river's lineage he'd come
From far Paionia, Troy's war to wage.
     Eleven days he'd had in Ilion,
     This twelfth, would be his very final one.

244

Troy's brave defender threw both spears at once,
Such was his skill, from both his hands they flew;
The shield stopped one yet with a grazing glance
The other slashed an arm and dark blood drew.
At Asteropaeus Achilles cast,
His ash lance flying fast on fury's wings,
It missed and in the river's bank stuck fast,
Yet then with sword he deadly purpose brings.
The man of Troy tried, thrice, to pull the spear
Of lord Achilles out for his defence.
Again, in vain, and this try cost him dear:
The dark lord's blade gave to him death's silence.
       Achilles stripped his armour boasting thus:
        "Those river born could not match sons of Zeus."

245

He left the corpse sprawled on the stream swept sands
And pulled his spear out from the river's bluff.
Now others fell there at Achilles hands
More would have died but Xanthus cried: enough!
The river's voice rose from heaving depths,
Complaining that his flows were crammed with dead.
He told Achilles: "Turn your tide of deaths
Back to the plain." In answer, swift, he said:
"Scamander, this will be as you command
But now I will not cease, for I must kill,
Till all who're left, behind Troy's walls I've crammed
And faced down Hector with my deadly skill."
       He cast death's curse about him as he'd vowed,
       Until with blood the river's currents flowed.

246

Scamander called out to Apollo: "Shame!
For Zeus commanded—these you should protect,
Till evening brought down darkness to the plain,
Yet here Achilles many lives has wrecked."
Then from the river bank that dark lord leapt
Into those middle waters, whirling deep.
Scamander then with boiling anger swept
Those dead to shore, in shadowed realms to sleep,
And those who lived he hid within his depths.
Waves mounted then against Achilles' shield,
With desperate strength he seized an elm which stretched
Above those waters, yet he felt it yield,
      Its roots tore up, then as a tangled mass
      Stopped those raging currents from their task.

247

From that whirlpool then Achilles ran,
And yet Scamander would not let him be,
Though from destruction, there, the swift lord sprang,
Dark waters rose in hope of victory.
Though like an eagle, black, he sped away,
The raging torrent rushed in wild pursuit,
He turned and tried to hold its surge at bay,
It beat him, tearing at him head and foot.
Achilles wearied, groaning to the sky,
Calling on the gods in his despair.
In midst of battle he knew he should die,
And not find worthless death in this god's lair.
      Poseidon heard him and Athene too,
      She came beside him promising rescue.

248

Achilles sped then with his strength renewed,
Though still Scamander raged at Pelion.
Simoeis, he called to aid his feud
And with his currents drown the mighty one.
Both thus rose into a boiling crest,
Filled with blood and dead that crimson wave;
Crowned with murmuring foam it downwards pressed,
To pull Achilles to a stagnant grave.
Yet Hera, fearing for him, cried out loud
And begged Hephaestus there to intervene
And use his fire to sear that watery shroud
Whilst she whipped wind to scorch the whirling stream.
  Consuming trees and corpses, fierce it came,
  And on the river's surge cast down its flame.

249

The hot blast burned the river's strength away.
He called on both the gods that work to cease;
Conceding now must come Achilles day,
Thus from the flaming torment begged release.
For Xanthus' lovely stream was scorched by fire
As when black cauldrons boil as flames leap high;
Scamander begged that Hera's son retire
And waited while the goddess made reply.
Hera, of the white arms, told her son
To quench his fires—then lovely waters ran
Back down their courses when the flames had gone,
And both gods rested, leaving Ilion.
  But on the others now that burden fell,
  And war-wards they the winds of hate compel.

250

Zeus on Olympus sat then, well amused,
To see the gods below, in hate, collide.
Athene there by Ares was abused
Called dog-fly, stirring trouble far and wide.
He stabbed against her aegis with his spear,
But that will not, to fire from Zeus, give way.
Athene took a large stone lying near
And felled him—huge upon the plain he lay.
On seven acres was his prone form spread,
Athene laughed in triumph at his pain,
Whilst Aphrodite from the conflict led
The god, until he, sense and strength regain.
      But Hera saw them leave and in pursuit
      Sent fair Athene, swift, in hot dispute.

251

Athene drove a blow into the breasts
Of Aphrodite, causing her to lie
With Ares, injured, out of those contests.
Thus willful Hera claimed her victory.
Then the other gods were stirred to act;
Poseidon told Apollo: "Bring to mind,
When with Laomedon we made a pact
And how he broke those oaths, which all should bind.
You herded all his beasts. I built his walls,
A year we laboured for a stated hire,
At season change when time of payment falls,
His voiding of that contract earned our ire.
      His threat to strip our ears and make us slaves
      Calls down our vengeance on these Trojan knaves."

252

Apollo answered: that he would not fight
For sake of mortals, who must fall as leaves,
He told Poseidon: "Leave them to their plight,
To war unaided, finding what fate weaves."
Then Artemis, his sister, scolding, spoke:
"To yield, you give him victory entire;
Posedon wins and soon you'll hear him boast
That you were no match for his warlike ire."
Though he stayed silent, angry Hera rose
And caught her by the arms and boxed her ears;
Thus Artemis then fled amid those snows
Which crown Olympus, weeping bitter tears.

      Her mother Leto gathered up her bow
      And arrows, fallen on the earth below.

253

Hermes also from the fight withdrew,
And Leto followed Artemis back home.
Zeus gave comfort asking why she flew,
Distressed, to kneel now by his great bronze throne.
She told him why and how the great gods fought,
Apollo, meanwhile, went to Ilion
Concerned lest its defences came to naught,
Stormed prematurely by the Greek's great son.
Elsewhere Achilles brought great sorrow down
On Trojans as the aged Priam watched,
Who going to the gateway of the town
Ordered its great doors to be unlatched,

      So back from fighting all his men might flee,
      Safe in siege, yet robbed of victory.

254

And as they fled, Achilles followed fast,
But then Apollo sprang to Troy's defence,
He said to Agenor: "Stand till the last,
To bear that storm of death which looms, immense."
Antenor's son then mused on what to do,
For if he ran he knew that he must die.
Then, god inspired, he stood, a Trojan true,
To fight the dread Achilles he must try.
Thus as a leopard, cornered, with no fear
He raised his weapon as the hunter came
And as he neared he loosed his deadly spear,
Which struck a greave, near wounding with its aim.
   Achilles' mother's gift stopped any hurt
   That spear rebounded, landing in the dirt.

255

Peleus' son then made a deadly spring
At god like Agenor, but was denied!
For lord Apollo caused dense mist to cling
About the Trojan standing at his side.
He sent him back to safety, then he stood
Before Achilles, formed as Agenor;
Thus disguised, towards Scamander's flood,
He ran and drew the dark lord from the war.
The swiftest mortal's speed could never match
That of the god, across the wheat rich plain;
His ruse then gave Troy's guards the time to latch
The gates, thus safe behind them all remain.
   He there beguiled that lord who brought Troy death
   Whilst all gained refuge, gasping hard for breath.

Book 22

256

So to the city, Trojans ran like fawns
And dried their sweat and drank, and slaked their thirst;
Then from Troy's mighty ramparts poured their scorns,
Inviting Greeks below to do their worst.
Yet fate held Hector, shackled, standing fast,
Before the city at the Scaian gates.
Far off, Apollo showed himself at last
To lord Achilles, mocking, how the fates
Had led him very far from Ilion.
Deeply vexed, the dark lord spoke with ire
Of promised deaths that god had stolen from
His spear, those fate had destined for the pyre.
      In haste he turned his flying steeds around
      Back to those walls, where Hector stood his ground.

257

Aged Priam first beheld the sight
Of his dread coming, shining like the star
Called Orion's dog which autumn bright
Outshines all others in the sky by far.
Such was the flare of bronze which girt that chest,
That elder groaned to see Achilles come
And begged great Hector not to seek the test
Of single combat with that deadly one
Who'd made such desolation of his sons.
He said how fleeting was that sorrow brought
By all their deaths compared to that which comes!
If Hector dies then all Troy comes to naught.
      He begged his noble son there to give way,
      To gain the place where hope and safety lay.

258

Then Priam prophesied what ills would fall
Upon his house, if Hector's sword was stilled;
With sons destroyed and daughters from his hall
Dragged captive, and their infant children killed.
Then last of all, himself, by dogs ripped raw
Before Troy's gates; ignobly, life thus torn
From him unlike from young cut down in war,
Their corpses youth's full freshness would adorn.
They kept their beauty while the old looked sad,
Grey beards defiled and all laid bare to see.
He tore his hair, his wife, in mourning clad,
Wept tears of death for his mortality.
       She cried to Hector, fight, your duty calls,
        Beat back dark, feared, Achilles from these walls.

259

Mother, father, both in tears called out,
But could not move the spirit of their son;
For Hector with his spear then hoped to rout
Achilles, who relentlessly came on.
He waited as a snake within his hole
So filled with evil poisons, that his mind,
Envenomed with dark fury, rules his soul
And coiled malignant waits: his death to find.
Yet deeply troubled to his heart he spoke,
And sloped his shining shield against the wall:
"If I give way as champion of my folk,
It shames my house, and ruin comes to all."
       He mused on every way to save the day
        And what would be, and what the world would say.

260

Achilles, as the lord of battles came,
To Hector, with his armour blazing bright
As sunlight when the dawn's immortal flame
Consumes the misty veils of fleeing night.
He held aloft the mighty Pelian spear,
And Hector trembled as he saw him come;
He left the gates and fled as he came near
In dread and fear, from Peleus' great son.
In pursuit, Achilles like a hawk,
Swooped effortless as though to seize a dove;
They passed the watch point where old sentries walk
And then the fig which juts out from above.
  They passed the two sweet springs, one hot, one cold
  Where maidens washed their robes in days of old.

261

A great man fled! A better man pursued!
In contest there, to win no common prize
Of ox hide or some festal beast, subdued;
'The victor here wins life, the loser dies'.
The two swept thrice around Troy's towering wall,
The gods looked down, amongst them great Zeus mourned,
He pondered yet—would Hector live or fall,
He knew the fates desired his life suborned.
Grey-eyed Athene asked her father this:
Did he defy the will of destiny?
For Hector's time had come to sink with Dis
Into those realms which hold eternity.
  Zeus made clear he would not stand before
  The fates' decree, nor bend immortal law.

262

Athene thus descended to fulfil
Fates' purpose, from those clouded mountain peaks;
Whilst on the plain Achilles ran to kill,
'There Hector's life his raging anger, seeks'.
Thus, as a mountain dog which tracks a fawn,
Which flushed from cover, may not then escape,
Dread Achilles came, relentless, on
And kept him from the safety of the gate.
The two were linked as figures in a dream,
When he pursuing ran but could not reach
The fleer, fleeing, in that nightmare deme
With no escape for fate bound each to each.
   Hector, briefly, then escaped his death
   For lord Apollo gave him strength and breath.

263

Achilles held Greek' spears and arrows back
For he alone must win the Trojan prize,
But then, four times, they'd passed the welling brook,
Thus father Zeus must judge on one's demise.
In golden scales he placed their portioned fate
And Hector's death-day dragged the balance down;
Thus Lord Apollo stood aside to wait,
For noble Hector there must fight alone.
Athene told Achilles then to hold
While she tricked Hector there to face his foe;
Thus in disguise as Deiphobus, bold,
She said: "We two will into battle go."
   False filled with courage, Hector thus will fight,
   Beguiled by hopes which bring eternal night.

264

Thus Hector turned and said to that dark lord,
That he would stand, but asked him first to vow
The victor would full honours there accord
To he who fell, and back to friends allow.
Achilles, looking darkly at him, said:
That there could be no oaths between those two,
And promised one must live soon with the dead,
That he would claim in blood all payments due.
He threw his spear but watchful Hector knelt
Whilst scything bronze above his shoulder flew;
Avoiding death that deadly lord had dealt,
But great Athene gave him cause to rue.
    She placed the spear back in Achilles hands,
    Thus, there, rearmed his deadly foeman stands.

265

Hector then, in hope, his missile threw,
It struck the centre of Achilles shield
And though the spear had winged there fast and true
It sprang back from the boss, which did not yield.
He stood discouraged, with no lance to hand
And then asked Deiphobus for his spear.
Yet he was nowhere near and that command,
Unfilled, revealed that Hector's death was near.
Though condemned he knew that he must try
To fight with glory, meeting manhood's test.
He drew his sword to try his destiny
And like an eagle swooped on the Greek's best.
    Yet as he charged, death's lord: Achilles, came
    In fury to conclude their deadly game.

266

To guard his chest, in front, the Greek chief bore
His god wrought shield, his head crowned with that helm
Four horned and golden fringed which like a star
Shone like Hesper, queen of heaven's realm.
He looked to find some weak point for his spear,
For splendid armour guarded Hector there—
That stripped from him Achilles held so dear:
Patroclus, who was lost, in Hades' lair.
Then through Achilles' form cold fury ran;
He drove his spear hard through poor Hector's neck
And brought to closure then his earthly span,
Thus with one thrust Troy's hopes all lay in wreck.
      The dying lord heard dark Achilles swear,
      That dogs and vultures, soon, his corpse would tear.

267

As his life ebbed then Hector made a plea
For honour's ransom and his death won rite;
In rage, Achilles said his destiny
Would be defilement; Troy would view that sight.
Through this, the dying lord said he'd be cursed,
The gods would see that he too was destroyed;
His soul then in death's silence was immersed,
He sank down into Hades' shadowed void.
Then lord Achilles spoke, as though he lived,
And said to Hector: "Death to all must come,
Frail mortals from eternal years are sieved
By fates who choose how long we see the sun."
      He pulled his spear out from dead Hector's neck
      And stripped the armour from his blood soaked flesh.

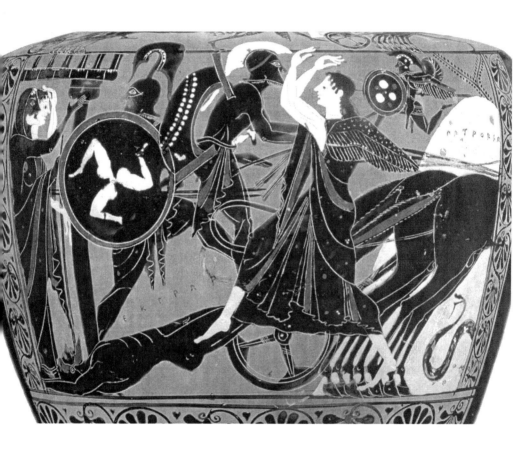

Achilles drags the body of Hector behind his chariot.

268

Then others of the Greeks came up to gaze
Upon the beauty of that silent form,
Each stabbed the body with a vengeful blade
As Hector lay defenceless and forlorn.
For all remembered when he'd fired their ships
And they stood back in fear as on he came;
But then these words came from Achilles lips
As Hector lay despoiled and wrapped in shame.
Let's ask the Trojans if they'll come to fight,
Or leave the city now their hero's gone.
His mind in conflict mused upon the plight
Of Patroclus, with death rites still not done.
      He ordered victory songs and swift return,
      So in the pyre his friend could, nobly, burn.

269

Achilles thought then, how to shame his foe;
Then pierced his heels and drew strong hide thongs through
And bound them to his cart with head laid low,
Then drove the chariot forward in full view
Of all who stood on Ilion's walls to see.
A dreadful sight, with steeds whipped up to run,
And Hector dragged to show that victory
Was won for Greece by its most dreaded son.
His mother then looked down in unbelief
And tore her hair, and rent her shining veil;
His father groaned, the people wailed in grief,
To see that head defiled, that corpse so pale.
      Then Priam tried to storm the gates of Troy
      And go to offer ransom for his boy.

270

The old man mourned and all the people wept,
While Hecuba, soft, led in sorrow's song
Her women for her child who ever slept
In Hades now amid war's fallen throng:
Those Greeks and noble brothers born of Troy.
She, now, in sorrow, dwelt among the dead
And sat in shadow, drained of hope and joy,
For Atropos had cut life's noblest thread.
Yet Hector's wife, within, had not yet heard
As there she worked to weave a bright red robe;
She ordered servants: "Have a bath prepared,"
As soon her husband home from fighting, strode.
      Then at the walls she heard the mourning grow,
      She dropped the shuttle; terror filled her now.

271

She called her maidens, those with lovely hair,
To come with her to see what was amiss,
For Hector's mother, crying in despair,
She'd heard with other voices in sadness.
Her pounding heart beat strong as though to burst,
Her limbs were frozen thinking evil near,
In madness then she ran as someone cursed
Outside, onto the walls, with mounting fear.
There she saw her dearest husband dragged
By foul Achilles, like some god of night.
Her breath rushed out, her knees beneath her sagged;
She fell and gasped, despairing at his plight.
      For death had come and taken all her joy
      Thus now she raise her voice, in dirge, for Troy.

272

Andromache thus mourned, for Hector lost:
Gone to the house of death beneath the earth,
For as a widow, now she saw the cost
To that young son to whom she'd given birth.
Astyanax, to him they gave that name
'Lord of the City' called for Hector, brave,
Defender of their walls of valiant fame;
Who now could not his son from sorrow save.
Before, the finest things of Troy he'd had
But hence, an orphan's portion he must take,
And he must suffer much, in mourning clad
As his dear father rotted near Troy's gate.
  Then back she ran, the waiting clothes to burn,
  And all Troy's women mourned for her in turn.

Book 23

273

Returning to their ships the warriors went,
Achilles though, held back his Myrmidons.
They drove up to the pyre, there to lament,
He led that mourning song of terror's sons.
Thetis stirred their passions and they wept,
The sands, their armour, glistening with tears.
Achilles said farewell with deep regret
And led the death chant and sad final prayers.
He said that what was promised was fulfilled,
With Hector slain, and twelve from Troy to die,
He thought once more to shame the one he'd killed
And laid him face down in the dust to lie.
     With war gear stripped, each then unyoked his steeds
     And then sat down to feast with Achilles.

274

With sundry oxen slaughtered for the feast
And many sheep, and bleating goats and swine,
Then roasted while rich blood ran from each beast
Into great cups as they prepared to dine.
Then all the lords brought great Achilles there,
With water heated so that he might bathe
To wash away the blood and his despair,
Then cleansed, to take Patroclus to his grave.
But anger filled him still and he declined
And vowed that he would stay, till on the pyre
He'd placed his friend, for sorrow filled his mind;
Then; for those comforts he had no desire.
     He bade them to the gloomy feast to dine,
     There, thousands took their fill of food and wine.

275

Thus satiated, all went off to sleep,
While on the beach Achilles paused, alone;
Where vaunting waves rode shore-wards from the deep
He lay, with many a mournful sigh and groan.
Then as he drifted off in fitful dreams
The ghost of dead Patroclus came and spoke,
To beg those funeral rites and fire which cleans
The soul to enter Hades with its folk.
He said: "Beyond the Styx at my next home,
They wait to great me, when flesh gives release;
Thus by the gates of death I still must roam,
Until by fire my torment gains surcease.
    Those rites performed would be a last farewell,
    For then amid the deathless shades I'll dwell."

276

Patroclus asked his friend one final boon;
To place their ashes in a golden urn
To be together, for his end came soon,
In death's bond as in life's they would return,
To lie together for eternity.
Achilles wondered why the dream had come
And said as his ghost wished, all things would be;
He tried then to embrace the spectral one,
But as he did the spirit, underground
Returned like vapour, leaving a thin cry.
Achilles started, waking at that sound
And spoke in wonder at this last goodbye.
    He rose and roused the Myrmidons to mourn
    As night gave way to rosy fingered dawn.

277

Then mighty Agamemnon orders gave,
For men with mules to search the wooded hills
And bring down timber for that last conclave,
Where sacred fire the funeral rite fulfils.
Mighty oaks were felled for that great mound,
Hewn by the thin edged bronze, and dragged in place.
The Myrmidons then drove their chariots round
And bore Patroclus to the pyre, apace.
Well armoured thousands brought him to his rest
And covered him with locks cut from their hair,
Achilles laid the friend who he'd loved best
Upon his final bed, then in despair
  He cut a lock, grown long, for Spercheius,
  Then spoke to that far river of his loss.

278

He said: "The vow I made will be in vain—
A lock be cut, when I had won safe home;
It seemed that now forever I'll remain
Here doomed by war, far from my father's throne."
But as that river god could not fulfil
His wish, and then he knew he'd not return,
He placed the lock in his friend's hand, so still;
And with his lords prepared the pyre to burn.
A hundred feet its base stretched, squarely made.
Then round the corpse he placed fat sheep and kine
And oil and honey sweet, around it laid
With horses and two dogs of his, from nine.
  With evil bronze the captive twelve from Troy
  Were slain, and placed for fire's wrath to destroy.

279

Achilles groaned and called by name his friend:
"Patroclus: laid in Hades house, farewell!
As those things promised to you at your end
Have been fulfilled, contented you must dwell."
Then though he tried, the pyre refused to light,
For there was one more thing he had to do,
He made a prayer and watched the wood ignite
For Boreas and Zephyrus then blew,
Brought by Iris from their stormy homes;
They swept in roaring blast across the sea,
They crossed the Troad, where the death god roams,
To light that flame which sets the bound soul free.
      Then from a golden bowl Achilles poured
      A last libation to the fallen lord.

280

All night long the funeral flames burned high
And great Achilles mourned, stood near that fire
Until the last star vanished from the sky
And dawn's new saffron mantle touched the pyre.
Then as the flames died down the winds returned
Across the Thracian waters to their home;
In torment, 'mid the moaning swell they churned,
Then lord Achilles sat, exhausted, down.
Sweet sleep then took him, till that all skilled son
Of Atreus arrived, and dreams disturbed,
Achilles woke and as the task was done
Asked wine be poured to cool the fiery bed.
      Then from cold ash they took those last remains
      From where Patroclus perished in the flames.

281

Achilles ordered that the bones in gold
Should lie until his own had joined them there.
The urn was veiled and earth piled high to hold
Those remnants waiting in their sacred lair.
All turned to go but were commanded, stay!
Achilles, then brought prizes for the games:
Cattle, tripods, cauldrons, iron grey,
Fine horses, waiting with their well oiled manes.
Fair girdled women, faultless with their hands,
And gold as rich rewards for all his peers;
He then called first, those lords from many lands
To try their hands as worthy charioteers.
      Yet from that contest he himself withdrew
      As his immortal horses as wind flew.

282

While lord Achilles chose a turning post,
Wise Nestor gave advice to his dear son:
Antilochus, of those sure skills which most
Ensured the coming contest would be won.
The lots were drawn, and of them his was first,
Eumelus followed, Menelaus then,
Meriones fourth and last and worst
Diomedes the best of all those men.
All raised their whips and then the horses sped,
Across the flat they ran with streaming manes,
All strained, at first those of Eumelus lead,
Diomedes then second at his reins.
      Panting hard his stallions tried to pass
      The leader's steeds, to show their breed and class.

283

In anger then, from swift Diomedes,
Apollo struck away his well held whip.
In tearful anger there he watched the steeds
Of Eumelus, with ease, his own outstrip.
Athene saw the deed and with her hands
Restored the whip so once more he might drive
And coax his horses fast with soft commands.
On went that vengeful goddess to deprive,
Eumelus of his lead in that swift race;
She smashed his yoke and as the pole dragged high
It threw him spinning, landing on his face;
Though injured, he held in his anguished cry.
   Diomedes' swift stallions took the lead,
   Yet Menelaus chased him at great speed.

284

Then Menelaus coaxed his flying two
With threats, and thus they hastened in their fear.
Antilochus drove, reckless, to pursue
And to the son of Atreus grew near.
There where the road grew narrow he gave way,
And cursed the son of Nestor as he passed,
Then urged his horses on without delay
To try to catch the leaders, flying fast.
The Argives tried to make out through the dust
Who lead the race, and spoke in hot dispute,
Until Achilles told them: "Put your trust
In what you see as now they end their route."
   Diomedes came first, the race to win,
   Antilochus, through skill, just after him.

285

Third Menelaus, then Meriones,
The fifth to finish, of them was the best.
In pity thus proposed great Achilles,
The second prize should now go to the last.
Antilochus there spoke up angrily,
And said that: "You have steeds and maids, and gold."
Achilles smiled on him and said that he
Would give a corselet won in warfare bold,
From Asteropaeus it had been stripped,
Made of wrought bronze, with overlay of tin;
Eumelus with great joy took up the gift
Which then Automedon brought out to him.
      Yet bitter in defeat, lord Menelaus,
      Spoke in anger to Antilochus.

286

Though Menelaus sourly spoke, of guile,
Antilochus gave generous reply,
And offered from his winnings to resile
And give him other gifts with those to lie.
With anger tempered by the young man's grace,
The mare was kept by him as was his right,
That lord took up the third prize in its place
And Meriones last, the gold coins bright.
Thus the jar, the fifth prize, then remained.
Achilles gave it Nestor, who in joy,
Remember times long past and other games
Where he had won, as others did at Troy.
      Amongst the Argives there, thus honoured,
      He called down blessings on Achilles head.

287

The prizes for the boxing then were brought,
A jenny yet unbroken, as the first.
A goblet for the second in that sport
Then two came forward, in those skills well versed.
Epeius, Euryalus then stood,
With belts on waists and fists wrapped round with thongs,
They strode into the circle seeking blood,
To see to whom the victory belongs.
With one blow Euryalus was felled,
Peering carelessly above his guard;
He spat out blood while his opponent held
Him, picked up fast, while dazed, from off the ground.
  Thus set by Epeius back on his feet
  He took the gold, contented in defeat.

288

The painful wrestling was the third event,
With a great tripod for the winner set,
A woman skilled in weaving there was sent
As second prize; she, would the loser get.
Telamonian Ajax then arose,
Huge in size and strong above the rest,
A second man, well skilled, that challenge chose,
Odysseus stood, to find out who was best.
The two girt up and hooked their heavy arms,
Then backs cracked as the straining limbs pulled hard,
Each grappled, holding with taut sinewed palms,
Slow time went by yet sweat from both men poured.
  The crowd grew restless at the long impasse,
  But neither could the other's strength outclass.

289

Then Ajax heaved and lifted, as he grasped,
Odysseus scythed a leg behind his knee,
And down to earth that great opponent crashed;
Three falls were needed though, for victory.
A second fall, both crashed down, lying close,
Yet Ajax, this time, gained the cherished point,
But at the third encounter one must lose
So lord Achilles made the two conjoint
In victory there, the prizes thus were shared.
Then for the foot race all was then set out
And for it there the fleetest three prepared,
The lesser Ajax, and fresh from his bout:
   Odysseus, and with him Nestor's son,
   To test their speed with prizes to be won.

290

From the start, swift Ajax reached the front
With great Odysseus breathing down his back;
He closer ran, swift gaining in the hunt
And prayed for aid so he could close the gap.
Athene heard him, making light his feet,
And in that final sprint poor Ajax slipped,
Where dung was scattered, falling to defeat.
Thus the silver bowl Odysseus gripped,
While Ajax won the ox and wryly said:
"Whilst I stand here and spit out foul ox dung
The slower man to victory was lead,
Athene's hand assured that he has won."
   Antilochus came last and won the gold
   A talent's worth; which he was glad to hold.

291

Next, in armoured combat, two came out:
Diomedes and Ajax, huge, to dare,
For Sarpedon's fine armour in that bout
And Thracian sword, with silver nails, to share.
The prize awarded when the dark blood flowed.
In three encounters all looked on in fear,
Thrice Ajax stabbed and thrice the stout shield bowed,
Protecting Diomedes from that spear.
The son of Tydeus aimed at the neck
Of Ajax and the danger then was great;
The Argives called Achilles now to check
That contest, thus to save him from his fate.
  The sword was given to Diomedes;
  The armour split between them as they pleased.

292

Achilles brought a weighty lump of iron
For him to keep, who furthest it could throw.
Polypoetes, brave as some fierce lion,
Won it, beating mighty Ajax now.
Next the archer's prizes were displayed,
(A tethered pigeon must be hit to win),
Those: ten half axes, ten with double blades;
All chose lots, to see who would begin.
Teucer won first place and thus let fly
And cut the tether, thus the pigeon soared;
Whilst it circled high up in the sky
Meriones loosed a shaft which scored.
  The dove fell dead and thus he took the prize,
  Apollo helped him, promised sacrifice.

293

A spear and unfired cauldron then were brought
As prizes for the last of all the games.
All who threw the lance well, thus were sought
And up rose two amid those famous names.
Agamemnon, lord of all, would try,
And Meriones too, would test his spear.
Achilles spoke, the contest to deny,
For Agamemnon far outclassed all there.
He asked the king, his cauldron, to accept
And placed the spear in Meriones hands;
The king at once agreed, without regret,
Thus lances were not tested on those sands.

   Those funeral games there held for Patroclus
   Made last farewells in memory of his loss.

Book 24

294

The games broke up and each went to his bed,
Achilles stayed though, restless in his grief;
His heart still for his friend Patroclus, bled.
He mourned till dawn's pale fingers touched the beach,
Then yoking his great steeds he then prepared
To drag dead Hector thrice around the tomb,
Yet Lord Apollo from defilement spared
The corpse, as it was dragged amid that gloom.
Twelve days had passed since noble Hector died
And thus Apollo pleaded with the gods,
And wondered how it was that they denied
Those honours which a valiant death accords.
   Pale Hera then replied with angry words:
   That, mortal, Hector gained what he deserved.

295

Then father Zeus consoled her angry mind
And said: "Amongst the heroes Hector stood
Above those others of the human kind,
And by the gods especially was loved."
He told them: "They might not the body steal
As Thetis always by her son stayed close,
Yet if she came to him, he would reveal
How Priam's gifts may salve their present woes."
Storm-footed Iris sprang to take his word
From high Olympus to those silent deeps.
Whilst plunging down, the dark sea moaned and roared
That she should dare invade his inner keeps.
   She came to Thetis in her secret caves
   And bade her rise above those troubled waves.

296

Thetis mourned Achilles, soon to die,
Surrounded by her deathless Nereids;
The silver footed goddess questioned why
She must go where sorrow's need forbids.
Reluctantly, she took up her black veil
And Iris led her up into the light;
The peak of high Olympus then to scale
Above those cares which filled the day and night.
With words of comfort Hera greeted her
And put a golden goblet in her hand,
For all of the immortals were aware
Her son must shortly die in that far land.
      Then mighty Zeus spoke of the ill repute
      Which her son's actions gained in his dispute.

297

Zeus sent her to Achilles camp to say—
The gods frowned on him then, as through his ire
Hector still in vile dishonour lay;
Denied his rites upon the funeral pyre.
She told him Priam's ransom to accept;
Achilles, to the god's demands agreed;
Then Zeus sent Iris down to Troy to get
The aged king with all her urgent speed.
She told him there, bring gifts and she would send
The herald, Hermes, down to be his guide,
And not to fear as that god would defend
Him from all Greeks, who in the night came near.
      Priam told his sons: prepare a cart,
      And went to choose the gifts and soon depart.

298

He asked his wife what ransom he should take
But she cried out aloud, replying then,
And begged him stay in safety, for her sake
And not to seek that deadliest of men.
For he had slaughtered many of their sons,
And though her heart cried out for sweet revenge,
Her fear condemned she suffer all those wrongs
But Priam's heart accepted that challenge.
Thus he ordered all those sons still left
To load his cart with gifts for Achilles.
He took out robes and mantles from his chest
And clothes and gold, that mighty lord to please.
      Tripods, cauldrons, all were put in place
      A golden cup; given him by men of Thrace.

299

Thus Priam took the finest of his store,
Of treasures there, to ransom his dead son;
At those remaining then, he scolding, swore;
For Hector's life he'd exchange every one.
He drove the Trojans from his cloistered walks
Reviling all and saying:—"Outside fate,
Beyond our walls with deadly purpose stalks
To bring death soon to all; you need but wait!"
Helenus and Paris, Agathon,
Pammon and Antiphonus remained,
Polites there and Hippothous among
Those nine with Deiphobus, shame had gained.
      Those sons, with Dios last, were still alive
      And won disgrace because they yet survived.

300

Now Priam gave them orders, speaking rough:
"Make haste my wicked children, my disgrace."
He called them liars, dancers, in rebuff,
And wished they all had died in Hector's place.
Thus they in terror brought the wagon out
And yoked the mules and brought out all the spoils,
And loaded them upon its beams so stout,
Then to the chariot's yoking turned their toils.
Then Hecuba came out with honeyed wine,
That Priam might libation make to Zeus,
And send up prayers and ask him for a sign
To prove Achilles yet would keep their truce.
   The lord of all the councils heard him pray
   And sent down a black eagle straightaway.

301

Then as the bird swept through the city square
The people's hearts were lifted, all were glad;
His kinsmen though lamented, in despair,
As Priam went into the wild Troad.
Idaeus, the herald, drove the team
Which hauled the wagon with the king's ransom
And both by father Zeus above were seen,
Who sent down Hermes his beloved son;
To guide the two among the hollow ships.
In form as a young man the winged god came
As clouded night brought down the day's eclipse;
Priam's choice was—fly or there remain.
   The kindly god came fast and took his hand,
   And asked him where he went in that dark land.

302

He offered then to aid the aged two
And spoke to both of all the dangers there,
Yet by his form, a god's will Priam knew,
And through that knowledge vanished all despair.
He asked the youth then of his lineage,
And Hermes claimed to be a Myrmidon,
"As henchman to Achilles," said the sage,
"Come tell me of the fate of my dear son."
He said: "Though Hector lies at his twelfth dawn
No worms feed on him, nor does flesh decay,
Nor is he damaged, dragged at night and morn
Around the tomb; all blood seems washed away.
　　　　It must be that the gods protect your son,
　　　　For in their hearts they love the fallen one."

303

On hearing this old Priam spoke in joy,
That Hector was remembered on death's stage
And offered his gold goblet to the boy
To be his guard and escort, as fair wage.
Hermes declined the gift but then agreed
To take the old men through the Grecian lines,
He sprang behind the horses with great speed
And took them far within the camp's confines.
They reached Achilles' shelter, then the youth
Pulled open its huge gates and let them in.
He then dismounted, bound to tell the truth,
Of who had sent him and his origin.
　　　　He told the two that Priam must alone
　　　　Go in and ask to take his dear son home.

304

Hermes went back to his mountain home
Leaving aged Priam to his fate;
For he must see Achilles all alone
And at his knees there humbly supplicate.
Unseen, the king came in and kissed his hand
And then with pleading words he begged release
For Hector's corpse, to where his pyre would stand,
For in its flames his mourning pain would cease.
All looked in wonder as the old king spoke
Before the one who'd slaughtered all his kin.
Then in Achilles, memories awoke
Of his old father waiting yet for him.
       He let go Priam's hand and both men wept
       For all the dead, in mourning and regret.

305

When sorrow's passions left them both at last
Achilles rose and spoke to the old king
In pity, for those evils of his past,
In wonder, that he came there, gifts to bring.
He said that both should put their grief aside
As life's thread this way by the fates was spun.
At Zeus' great door, two unlike urns abide—
One holds good, from one is evil won;
From both, the king of all the gods must choose,
Then mingle and bestow on each his fate;
Good fortune comes to some, while others lose
All riches and their loved ones come to hate.
       He spoke about the gifts of Peleus,
       So far away, he mourned the old king's loss.

Hector's body lies beneath the couch of Achilles as Priam begs for its return.

306

Achilles turned to Priam to recall
How he had brought great sorrow to his land,
And spoke of all his wealth, when lord of all,
The eastern kingdoms his dominion spanned.
He said that naught was gained from endless grief,
The heart's desire could not his son restore;
Yet Priam begged Achilles to be brief,
He could not rest till Hector's corpse he bore
Back to his home, to lie in honoured state.
He asked them all before that mighty lord
To take the ransom in his dear son's place,
That he might journey home with that reward.
  Achilles darkly spoke at what he'd heard,
  And said by pleas for haste, he'd not be stirred.

307

He told old Priam of the god's request:
That he should, willingly, the corpse restore,
But warned him not to hasten that behest
As sorrow's doubts still made his mind unsure.
In anger there, he may their laws transgress
And moved by rage, a supplicant destroy.
Priam thus obeyed, in great distress,
In fear that haste's desire would lose his boy.
Then Achilles bounded to the door
Like some great lion, with two henchmen close:
Automedon and Alcimus who bore
The gifts inside and all the steeds unyoked.
  They brought the ancient herald in, to sit,
  And all that ransom for a hero fit.

308

Inside the wagon two great cloaks were left
With one fine tunic, fitting as a shroud.
Achilles told his maids, with fingers deft
To wash the corpse and then, without, make proud
That noble form, thus soothing Priam's heart.
With all anointings done the mantled form
Achilles lifted so they might depart.
Then gently to his litter he was borne,
By those strong arms, which caused him not to live;
Achilles groaned and called his dead friend's name:
"Patroclus, do not anger that I give
Great Hector back to his sire's rightful claim."
      The dark lord then went back to take his seat
      And told old Priam, "Stay this night and eat."

309

He said that fair Niobe stopped to eat
With all her children laid among the dead:
"Thus now old sir, we two must take our meat,
At dawn, back through our ranks you will be led."
Achilles then sprang up and slew a sheep
And both his friends cut portions there, to roast;
Automedon set bread out with the meat:
Achilles serving as befits the host.
Priam gazed in wonder at that lord,
Whose size and beauty surpassed other men;
Achilles, in his turn, gave due accord
To that old king, who had such courage then.
      Priam asked them for a place to sleep,
      A boon denied for so long by his grief.

310

Achilles told his serving maids to make
A bed within the shelter of his porch,
Then they chose purple robes—soft fleeces take,
Outside to do his bidding, with a torch.
Priam, thus, was told to sleep outside,
Lest some Achaian coming in the night
Should see him and the secret then confide
To Agamemnon, of the old king's plight.
Achilles asked him then, how many days
Were needed to complete the funeral
Of Hector, as from war's relentless ways
He would abstain and from the fray keep all.
   Priam, for eleven days did ask
   For due completion of that solemn task.

311

He said: "That wood is needed from the hills,"
Nine days he asked to bring it, and to mourn.
"The tenth day, Troy, all funeral rites fulfils,
The next our grief his burial mound adorns.
Thus by the twelfth our army can return
To this sad conflict; fighting if we must."
Achilles made a promise to confirm
That all would happen as the old king wished.
The lords and great Achilles lay to sleep
And fair Briseis lay with him, in bed,
And outside Priam lay, in slumber deep,
Their guide planned how back home he might be led.
   Then Hermes came above his head and spoke:
   "While all sleep now come quick, your steeds to yoke."

312

Thus through that silent night they stole away,
And Hermes drove them through the camp until
They reached fair Xanthus at the break of day,
Now he could leave them there, beyond peril.
As dawn's soft yellow robe spread o'er the plain
They drove in lamentation up to Troy,
Where only fair Cassandra saw their train
And she cried out to all, bereft of joy:
"Come all you Trojans look on Hector, dead!
You, in the past would gladly watch him come
Alive from battle, when the Greeks had fled,
The noble saviour, then, of everyone."
      In sorrow past endurance all were held,
      As they beheld Troy's son, unparalleled.

313

First among the throng was Hector's wife
And by her side his honoured mother stood,
All greeted Priam, wracked by sorrow's strife,
Then mourning tears flowed down in grief's full flood.
His mother touched his head, then tore her hair,
And all before the gates would have remained
But that the old king said, that their despair
Must wait until the palace yard he'd gained.
All stood aside as they brought Hector in
And on a carved bed there his corpse was laid,
Beside him, seated, those who would begin
The song of sorrow for that noble brave.
      Andromache, those weeping singers led,
      Whilst cradling her peerless husband's head.

314

She cried: "My Hector, you have died so young
And leave me now a widow in your halls;
Your child will die, from Troy's high ramparts flung,
Or be enslaved, when soon our city falls.
Now all its people, deeply, grieve for you
And both your parents drink from sorrow's gourd,
You died in battle, far beyond my view,
With no last kiss for me, or close breathed word."
Then Hecuba took up that chant of woe
For Hector, dearest of her sons by far.
"Though death has come, may yet the gods bestow
Protection on you as they did in war.
     And though Achilles dragged you round the tomb
     You lie here fresh and perfect in this room."

315

Third and last of all fair Helen came,
To lead in lamentation that vast throng,
She spoke of Hector's kindness in her pain,
Of his fair words when others did her wrong.
The dearest of the brothers of her lord
She mourned, in sorrow, as her only friend,
Always gentle, never harsh in word,
When others blamed her, he spoke to defend.
She said that Alexandros brought her here,
Before she came, she wished that she had died,
For now her exile reached its twentieth year
Since she had come with Paris as his bride.
     She spoke in tears and grieved for both of them,
     For death had claimed the noblest of all men.

316

Then Priam spoke to all the braves of Troy
And told them to bring timber without fear.
He knew the Argive hordes would not destroy
His men in ambush, ranging far and near.
He told them how Achilles, near the shore,
Had promised truce until the twelfth day came;
Thus filled with grief yet safe from threat of war
They ranged the hills in wagons, wood to gain.
Nine days were spent to bring the timber in
And build before Troy's walls a mountain pyre.
Then as the tenth dawn came his weeping kin
Placed noble Hector on its wooden spire.
     They watched him high amid those cleansing flames,
     Fire frees the spirit while poor flesh it claims.

317

Then as the young dawn's rosy fingers swept
Across the earth at that eleventh dawn,
The people gathered by the fire which wept
With flames unending, round the hero's form.
With gleaming wine they quenched those ceaseless flames;
Then all his kinfolk gathered Hector's bones
And in a golden casket his remains
Were laid in purple robes beneath old stones
Which marked his grave. While watchmen looked around,
In fear the waiting Greeks would break their word,
Then all departed from that burial mound
To Priam's house to feast their greatest lord.
     Horse-breaking Hector sleeps with honour vast,
     Such was his funeral there, in ages past.

Glossary of names

When I first read the Iliad I often found it confusing. I realised that this was due in large measure to the many alternative names that are used. For example Paris is also Alexandros, the Greeks can be Danaans, Argives, Achaians or men of Argos. Major characters are also not infrequently referred to by the ancestral name (patronymic); epithets are frequently used to signify the character, these are included in brackets after the name in the list below. All this of course is necessary to maintain freshness in a long narrative poem which otherwise could become boring due to constant repetition of the same name. Many of the minor characters who, for example, are identified in the Iliad and then rapidly killed by one of the major characters, are omitted.

Acamus: King of the Thracians.

Achaians: The Greeks.

Achilles (Achilleus): (Peleus' great son). The greatest of the Greek warriors.

Aeneas: Trojan prince, son of Anchises and Aphrodite. He must survive as he will ultimately lead the Trojans (and, in a subsequent epic, found Rome).

Agamemnon: (son of Atreus). The overlord of all the Greek chiefs. Importantly in the Iliad, his power was not absolute.

Aiantes: The name used when both Ajaxes act in conjunction.

Ajax: (Telamonian Ajax. The greater Ajax.)

Ajax: (Ajax son of Oileus. The lesser Ajax.)

Anchises: Aged king of Dardania and father of Aeneas (the Dardanians are Troy's allies).

Andromache: Hector's wife.

Antenor: Dardanian elder statesman, noted councillor and conciliator.

Antilochus: Noted warrior on the Greek side and friend of Achilles. Nestor's eldest son.

Aphrodite: (the lady of Cyprus). Goddess of love and supporter of Troy.

Apollo: (Phoebus Apollo). God of prophecy and divination. God of healing, and destruction via his silver bow. Supported Troy.

Arcadie: (Arcadia). Mountainous province in Greece.

Ares: God of war and supporter of Troy.

Ariadne: The daughter of Minos, king of Crete.

Artemis: Goddess of hunting and women. Supporter of Troy.

Astyanax: Sobriquet of Hector's son Scamandrius (it means Lord of the City).

Athene: (Hate's goddess, Sorrow's lady: Hate). Supported the Greeks.

Atreidae: Patronymic for Agamemnon and Menelaus.

Atreus: Father of Agamemnon and Menelaus.

Atropos: One of the three Fate's, she cuts the thread of life bringing death. Clotho spun the thread and Lachesis determined its length.

Automedon: Warrior friend of Achilles and father of Neoptolemus.

Briseis: Concubine of Achilles. Her appropriation by Agamemnon leads to Achilles anger and withdrawal from the conflict. Though a pawn in the narrative, her treatment is a major determinant of the events which follow.

Calchas: Greek seer. His explanation of the cause of the plague being rained down on the Greeks by Apollo led to Agamemnon surrendering Chryseis.

Cheiron: Centaur who lived in a cave on mount Pelion. At the wedding of Peleus and Thetis (Achilles parents) his gift to Peleus was a great ash spear.

Chryses: Priest of Apollo, father of Chryseis.

Chryseis: Taken captive by the Greeks and given to Agamemnon, restored to her father at the start of the Iliad.

Cnossus: (Knossos). Capital of Minos, king of Crete.

Cronus: King of the Titans, father of Zeus.

Daedalus: Master craftsman who built the maze in which 'the Minotaur' was shut away, and the dancing floor for Ariadne.

Danaans: One of Homer's names for 'The Greeks'.

Dardanians: Trojans.

Deiphobus. Son of Priam. Took command of Trojan forces after Hector's death.

Demeter: The Greek goddess of corn and thus of life.

Diomedes: Notable Greek warrior. Son of Tydeus, king of Argos.

Diores: Trojan warrior.

Dolon: Trojan scout killed by Diomedes.

Enyalius: A war god on Troy's side.

Euphorbus: One of the greatest of the Trojan warriors, killed by Menelaus.

Eurypylus: Ally of the Trojans and leader of the Mysians. Killed by Neoptolemus.

Gargarus: The peak of mount Ida.

Glaucus: Trojan Ally. Co-leader of the Lycians with Sarpedon, his cousin.

Hades: The underworld and also the name of the god who ruled it (also called Aidoneus).

Hebe: Goddess of youth: she ministers to the needs of other gods.

Hecatomb: A great public sacrifice. The word denotes a great quantity of sacrificial animals or victims.

Hector: The greatest of the Trojan warriors.

Hecuba: Priam's wife and mother of Hector.

Helen: (The fair one).

Helenus: Son of Priam, killer of Deipyrus.

Helicaon: Mountain in Boetia, abode of the Muses and site of springs sacred to them. Immortally described by Keats in his "Ode to a Nightingale" as 'the blushful Hippocrene'.

Hephaestus: The god of fire and metalworking. Lame from birth. Supporter of the Greek faction.

Hera: (The Owl eyed lady). The wife of Zeus who was determined that Troy would be destroyed.

Hermes: Herald and messenger of the gods, he supported the Greek side.

Hesper: The evening star (Venus).

Hypnos: The god of sleep.

Iantes: The greater and lesser Ajax.
Ichor: This flowed in the veins of the gods instead of blood.
Ida: Mountain in Phrygia, favourite seat of Zeus.
Idaius: Priam's Charioteer.
Idomemeus: (Idomene). King of Crete, leading his contingent in support of the Greek cause.

Ilium or Ilion: Troy.
Imbrios: Priam's son in law, killed by Teucer.
Iris: Messenger of the gods.

Kebriones: Hector's Charioteer, killed by Patroclus.

Laertes: Father of Odysseus.
Laodice: The most beautiful of Priam's daughters.
Laomedon: Father of Priam.
Leto: Mother of Apollo and Artemis, a supporter of Troy.
Linus: A musician who was famous for his laments.
Lycaon: A son of Priam, killed by Achilles.
Lycians: Allies of Troy.

Machaon: Son of Asclepius and like him a noted healer.
Maeonia: Lydia in Asia Minor.
Menelaus: King of Sparta and Helen's husband. Also Agamemnon's brother.
Meriones: Notable Greek warrior, second in command of the Cretans.
Mycenae: City in southern Greece. Agamemnon's capital.
Myrmidons: The fearsome band of warriors commanded by Achilles.

Nereids: Sea Nymphs.
Nestor: (Geranian Nestor).

Oceanus: God of the great river of the same name, encircling the Earth. At this time the Earth was, of course, flat.

Odysseus: (he of many talents). King of Ithaca, noted for his skills in many fields.

Paeon: God of healing.

Paeonia: A land north of Macedonia.

Pandarus: Noted Archer on the Trojan side.

Paris: (Alexandros). Brother of Hector and seducer of Helen and thus the root cause of the Trojan war.

Patroclus: Beloved friend of Achilles, killed by Hector.

Peleus: Achilles' father.

Pelion: Mountain in Thessaly and home of the centaurs.

Periphras: Trojan herald.

Phegeus: Trojan, aide to Aeneas.

Phoenix: Aged tutor and comrade of Achilles.

Phrygia: Part of Asia Minor which included Troy.

Podarge: One of the Harpies. She mated in the form of a mare with Zephyrus to produce the immortal horses Xanthus and Balius.

Polydamas: Sage advisor of Hector. Hector, rashly, usually rejects his advice.

Polydorus: Priam's youngest son. Killed by Achilles.

Poseidon: (The shaker of the earth). God of the Sea, brother of Zeus and supporter of the Greek side.

Pramnian wine: Noted wine produced around Smyrna.

Priam: King of Troy.

Rhesus: Thracian chief, killed by Diomedes.

Sarpedon: Trojan. Most beloved of the gods, son of Zeus. Killed by Patroclus.

Scaian: Main gates of Troy.

Scamander: Name of Astyanax, Hector's son.

Scamandros: Chief river of Troy and the name of its river god.

Scyrus: Island near Euboia.

Simoes: Tributary of the Scamandros.

Socus: Trojan killed by Odysseus.

Styx: The main river of Hades over which Charon ferries the souls of the dead.

Talthybius: Herald and friend to Agamemnon.

Tartarus: The lower depths of Hades. The Titans and other immortal enemies of Zeus are imprisoned here.

Tethys: Wife of Oceanus.

Teucer: Notable archer, half brother to Ajax.

Thanatos: The god of death.

Themis: Goddess of custom and order.

Thersites: Greek rabble rouser of low status who was squashed by Odysseus.

Thetis: Mother of Achilles.

Tithonus: Dawn's husband.

Tiryns: City in Greece noted for its mighty walls.

Tlepolemus 1: Killed by Sarpedon. Leader of the men of Rhodes.

Tlepolemus 2: Killed by Patroclus.

Tydeus: Father of Diomedes.

Xanthus: Alternative name for the river Scamander also name of Immortal horse belonging to Achilles.

Zeus: (The king of gods, The chief Olympian, The Son of Cronos).

Illustrations